Typical and Atypical Child and Adolescent Development 2

Genes, Fetal Development and Early Neurological Development

This concise guide offers an accessible introduction to genes, fetal development and early brain development. It integrates insights from typical and atypical development to reveal fundamental aspects of human growth and development, and common developmental disorders.

The topic books in this series draw on international research in the field and are informed by biological, social and cultural perspectives, offering explanations of developmental phenomena with a focus on how children and adolescents at different ages actually think, feel and act. In this succinct volume, Stephen von Tetzchner explains key topics including: Genetic inheritance, evolution, heredity and environment in individual differences, fetal development, prenatal stimulation, methods of studying the brain, brain development, early and later plasticity, and brain organization and atypical development.

Together with a companion website that offers topic-based quizzes, lecturer PowerPoint slides and sample essay questions, *Typical and Atypical Child and Adolescent Development 2: Genes, Fetal Development and Early Neurological Development* is an essential text for all students of developmental psychology, as well as those working in the fields of child development, developmental disabilities and special education.

Stephen von Tetzchner is Professor of Developmental Psychology at the Department of Psychology, University of Oslo, Norway.

T0348095

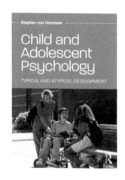

The content of this topic book is taken from Stephen von Tetzchner's core textbook *Child and Adolescent Psychology: Typical and Atypical Development*. The comprehensive volume offers a complete overview of child and adolescent development – for more information visit www.routledge.com/9781138823396

Topics from Child and Adolescent Psychology Series
Stephen von Tetzchner

The **Topics from Child and Adolescent Psychology Series** offers concise guides on key aspects of child and adolescent development. They are formed from selected chapters from Stephen von Tetzchner's comprehensive textbook *Child and Adolescent Psychology: Typical and Atypical Development* and are intended to be accessible introductions for students of relevant modules on developmental psychology courses, as well as for professionals working in the fields of child development, developmental disabilities and special education. The topic books explain the key aspects of human development by integrating insights from typical and atypical development to cement understanding of the processes involved and the work with children who have developmental disorders. They examine sensory, physical and cognitive disabilities and the main emotional and behavioural disorders of childhood and adolescence, as well as the developmental consequences of these disabilities and disorders.

Topics books in the series

Typical and Atypical Child and Adolescent Development 1
Theoretical Perspectives and Methodology

Typical and Atypical Child and Adolescent Development 2
Genes, Fetal Development and Early Neurological Development

Typical and Atypical Child and Adolescent Development 3
Perceptual and Motor Development

Typical and Atypical Child and Adolescent Development 4
Cognition, Intelligence and Learning

Typical and Atypical Child and Adolescent Development 5
Communication and Language Development

Typical and Atypical Child and Adolescent Development 6
Emotions, Temperament, Personality, Moral, Prosocial and Antisocial Development

Typical and Atypical Child and Adolescent Development 7
Social Relations, Self-awareness and Identity

For more information on individual topic books visit www.routledge.com/Topics-from-Child-and-Adolescent-Psychology/book-series/TFCAAP

Typical and Atypical Child and Adolescent Development 2

Genes, Fetal Development and Early Neurological Development

Stephen von Tetzchner

Routledge
Taylor & Francis Group

LONDON AND NEW YORK

Cover image: © SEBASTIAN KAULITZKI/SCIENCE PHOTO LIBRARY/Getty Images

First published 2023
by Routledge
4 Park Square, Milton Park, Abingdon, Oxon OX14 4RN

and by Routledge
605 Third Avenue, New York, NY 10158

Routledge is an imprint of the Taylor & Francis Group, an informa business

British Library Cataloguing-in-Publication Data
A catalogue record for this book is available from the British Library

Library of Congress Cataloging-in-Publication Data
A catalog record has been requested for this book

ISBN: 978-1-032-27384-6 (hbk)
ISBN: 978-1-032-26769-2 (pbk)
ISBN: 978-1-003-29245-6 (ebk)

DOI: 10.4324/9781003292456

Typeset in Bembo
by Apex CoVantage, LLC

Access the companion website: www.routledge.com/cw/vonTetzchner

Contents

Introduction

Development can be defined as an age-related process involving changes in the structure and functioning of humans and other species. Humans are complex beings who differ in many ways, differences that are related to biology, experiences and culture. The three parts in this topic book present two core developmental issues (genes and environment in development and brain development) and one **developmental phase** (the fetal period). They build on the models of development and the developmental way of thinking presented in Book 1, *Theoretical Perspectives and Methodology*. The three parts include both typical development, which is the most common course, with unimpaired functions and ordinary individual differences between children, and atypical development, which represents various degrees of unusual or irregular development, including the development of children and adolescents who have characteristics that fulfil the diagnostic criteria for one or several disorders, such as hearing impairment, autism spectrum disorder or anxiety.

Human development to maturity stretches over about 20 years, and most individual differences in physical and mental features and abilities do not emerge directly from a particular biological or environmental factor but rather as a result of **interaction effects**, where biological and environmental factors are moderated by one or several other factors. For example, the bases for children's early temperament are present at birth, but how children react in different situations and their development of personality traits depend on the positive and negative features of the environment. Importantly, this is not a one-way process: children are influenced by and influence their environments. Development is thus a *transactional process*, characterized by reciprocal influences between the child and the environment over time. The reader may find it useful to read Book 1, *Theoretical Perspectives and Methodology*, or the corresponding chapters in the complete book before reading the present book.

Part I Genes, Evolution, Heredity and Environment is about the basic processes of development. The genetic basis for human traits and abilities is the result of evolutionary processes (phylogeny). Knowledge about the genes' functions is crucial for understanding of the evolution of general human characteristics as well as abilities and traits that vary between people. Genes both enable and constrain development. They control reproduction and the overall structure of humans, and the transference of genes from parents to offspring contributes to biological continuity over generations. However, genes vary across individuals and they are therefore an important source of individual differences in development (ontogeny). Some gene variants do not support normal development, or represent vulnerability for developing physical or mental disorders. For example, the probability of developing anxiety disorder is higher when other family members present with this disorder. Inheritance is prominent also in everyday explanations of children's development: parents often claim that particular physical characteristics or personality traits are inherited from the father or from the mother, or from the grandfather or grandmother. However, developmental processes require environments with properties that enable development. Parents and other adults are concerned with the effects that a child's environment may have on his or her development, learning and well-being. In general, children are adaptable and show positive development in different environments, and some cope and show **resilience** in spite of growing up in environments with war or other forms of violence and atrocities that may hinder positive social experiences and learning.

Many studies seek to assess the role of individual genes and the relative influence of genes and environment on particular aspects of development, for example language, intelligence or emotional regulation. However, the main developmental issue is rather how genes and environment interact, how differences in a gene's DNA, nutrition and other features of the physical environment, and the social environment together influence these aspects of development. Neither genes nor environmental factors alone can explain the course of development: both are needed, and the scientific and practical problem is *how* they influence development. The state of the knowledge of this process will affect societies' possibilities of promoting positive development and reducing the risk of negative developmental outcomes.

There is increasing knowledge about the genetic bases of many disorders, but there is still no consensus regarding the precise role of nature and nurture in most abilities. How influences from genes and environment interact in development is still one of the most discussed issues in many areas of developmental psychology.

Clinical child and adolescent psychology is seeking to understand the biological and experiential bases for deviant development as well as resilience. Insights into the opportunities and constraints implied by a child's genes and environment are the basis for designing early and later intervention and training. The question of nature and nurture for various abilities and skills thus has significant practical implications.

Development starts when the sperm unites with an egg cell. *Part II Stimulation and Activity During Fetal Development* presents the giant developmental steps taking place over this period of about 40 weeks (when the child is born at term). The fetal period is unique with the transformation from a single cell to a human baby. It is a busy time, with regular periods in which the cells build the various parts of the body and functions start to merge, but it also includes periods where the development of the fetus is particularly vulnerable to disease or biochemical exposure. Much of the development in the fetal period is concerned with what is common to all humans, that is, with building a baby that can live and develop outside the mother's womb: breathing independently and being nourished through the mouth instead of through the mother's blood. At birth, the baby is ready to meet the physical and social world as an individual – although not yet an independent human being.

The developmental processes in the prenatal period are of great scientific interest because they enable the more interactive developmental processes after birth. The prenatal processes are biological rather than psychological and lay the foundation for perceptual, motor, cognitive, emotional and social development (see other topic books). However, even in this phase, the genetic basis does not alone determine a child's development; the genes and stimulation from the environment work together. The fetus develops sensory organs that start to function and an emerging motor control that develops further after meeting the gravitational forces of the outside world. The prenatal experiences and developmental processes may influence the course of development after the child is born.

The function of the central nervous system is an integrative part of developmental psychology. *Part III Brain Development* is about the development of the brain and the many functions processed in the brain. In spite of advanced technological developments, it is still difficult to find the way among the 86 billion nerve cells and their connections. In addition to measuring blood flow and electric currents in the brain, observations of children's actions, thinking and emotions are necessary for investigating brain functions.

The brain is central to all processes involved in children's adaptation and learning, both during the fetal phase and later. Experiences, learning and memory are represented in the brain in different ways. Compared with other species, the human brain is large relative to the size of the body, and the size of the human brain is one reason for the exceptional abilities and survival of human beings, and complex human societies. The brain has a biological basis that has developed through evolution and is transferred to the next generation through the genes. For the genes to have an impact on abilities that are grounded in the functioning of the brain, the genes' DNA must have an effect on processes that govern the development of the brain. Moreover, it is not a direct genetic influence: brain development depends on experience and activity and, like most developmental processes, is the result of interactions between genetic and environmental factors. Any minor or major new skill, experience or insight involves the organization of neuron groups and neurological processes. An individual's experiences may affect the thickness, height, length and weight of parts of the brain.

At birth, the brain is ready for the next phase of development. The development of brain structures and functions depends on experiences, and postnatal experiences differ qualitatively from the prenatal phase in the womb. It is an essential part of development where the brain structures and functions are becoming more fixed with age. For example, when the brain has developed the brain structures for the first language or languages, later languages have to be learned with the help of these structures. From a neurological perspective, early and later language learning are thus different processes.

Brain development illustrates both the complexity and the flexibility of human development. Insights into sensitive periods in postnatal development, such as the ease of learning language in the early compared with later years, are important both for understanding the significance of the child's experiences in different phases of development and as a basis for developing early childhood intervention.

Knowledge of the issues presented in this topic book is significant for *applied developmental science*. Insights into the developmental possibilities and constraints presented by a child's genes can imply a need for particular intervention measures. The fact that experience is important for brain development contradicts the belief that atypical development is predetermined, and it is a strong argument for providing early and later interventions to children showing developmental difficulties. In fact, **habilitation** and **rehabilitation** are based on the assumption that medical, educational and psychological measures will change the child's environment in a broad sense and thereby moderate or prevent a negative developmental course that a genetic mutation or chromosome abnormality might imply without such measures.

Some of the terminology used in developmental psychology may be unfamiliar to some readers. Many of these terms are highlighted in the text and can be found in the Glossary at the back of the book.

Part I

Genes, Evolution, Heredity and Environment

1

Phylogeny and Ontogeny

Human genes have emerged through evolution (phylogeny) and are one of the essential biological foundations for individual **development** (ontogeny). Genes allow information to be transmitted from one generation to the next so that the fusion of a human sperm cell and an egg (ovum) results in an individual with the particular mix of properties that distinguish humans as a species with two legs, the ability to walk upright, color vision and language. Thus, genes form the basis for *shared* human characteristics.

At the same time, every individual is genetically unique, with the exception of identical twins, who share their genetic makeup. In addition to the traits shared by all – or nearly all – human beings, genes carry the potential for the development of a wide range of traits that vary from individual to individual. It is this genetic basis that constitutes the *individual heritage* and forms the basis for discussions about the contributions of heredity and environment, or nature versus nurture, to **individual differences**, for example in musicality or **personality**.

Today, genes are believed to be involved in the development of many traits, including intelligence and **temperament**, as well as the disposition for developing obesity, language disorders or schizophrenia (Gottesman & Hanson, 2005; Rutter, 2006). Some genes affect development starting with the first cell divisions or at specific times during fetal life, while others first take effect late in adult life. Spontaneous **mutations** or errors in the division of certain **chromosomes** can occasionally occur, such as in the case of **Down syndrome** (see Table 3.1, p. 00). More than 2,000 genetic **syndromes** are known to exist, and there is reason to believe that many severe impairments and conditions of unknown cause are due to genetic predisposition.

DOI: 10.4324/9781003292456-2

However, there is a complex interplay between genes and environment. Knowledge about *how* genes control species-specific development and contribute to individual characteristics remains limited. A gene can function in a number of ways, and some genes affect the activity of other genes (Rutter, 2014). Therefore, finding that particular genes are associated with a given developmental anomaly does not necessarily reveal the underlying developmental mechanisms and consequently does not always make it possible to prevent or cure the anomaly.

2

Chromosomes and Genes

Chromosomes are thread-like structures that contain genes and are located inside the cellular nucleus. Human sperm and egg cells contain 23 chromosomes each. When they unite during conception, they form a single cell consisting of 23 pairs, or 46 chromosomes. With the exception of reproductive cells, or *gametes*, all of the body's cells thus normally contain 46 chromosomes. The arrangement in pairs applies to all but **sex chromosomes**: women have two X chromosomes, while men have an X and a Y chromosome (Figure 2.1). During cellular division, each of the genes on the 46 chromosomes is copied, and the genetic information is transferred to both new cells (except during the production of gametes, which consist of only 23 chromosomes). The chromosome structure is retained as well.

Genes are made up of **deoxyribonucleic acid**, DNA, which consists of long, helical threads that contain over a million different proteins in human beings. As each chromosome consists of about 1,000 genes, every cell contains approximately 23,000 different genes, and the genes in one cell can have a length of almost 2 meters. A **genome** represents all the DNA sequences of a single species (Gerstein et al., 2007). The most important property of DNA is to provide a model for producing **ribonucleic acid**, RNA, which performs a variety of functions inside the cell, controls the formation of new proteins and catalyzes chemical reactions in the body.

Alleles are genes that share the same location on the two chromosomes in a chromosome pair and control the same genetic characteristics. Alleles are not identical, and different individuals can carry different alleles in a pair of genes. This gives rise to individual differences (Gottlieb et al., 2006). Although specific genes may have a

DOI: 10.4324/9781003292456-3

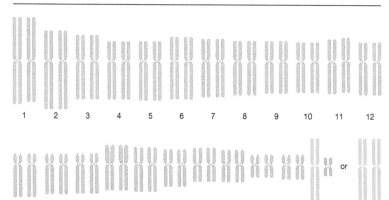

Figure 2.1 Human chromosomes.

There are **22 autosomal chromosome** pairs and two different pairs of sex chromosomes: one XY (male) and one XX (female).

particular task in the developmental process, it is rare that a characteristic is determined by a single gene. Even the eye color of the banana fly is the combined result of 13 genes. About 5,000 genes are involved in cellular maintenance and must therefore be expressed in all cells. Apart from minor variations, the same 5,000 genes are contained in all the cells of all species, but minute changes in the way these 5,000 genes interact allow for major structural differences. Moreover, there is no simple relationship between the number of genes two species have in common and the degree of similarity between them. For example, humans and mice share 99 percent of their genes, while humans and chimpanzees share 98.4 percent (Gottlieb et al., 2006). It is the way in which genes interact, rather than the presence of specific genes, that results in the differences between species.

3

Genetic Inheritance

Children get their genes from their parents. Inheritance in the genetic sense refers to the information transmitted to a human being or animal via the genes contained in the parent sperm and egg cell. The reproductive cells produced by an individual are not identical however. They only contain one chromosome from each of the 23 chromosome pairs, and the particular chromosome that is passed on is random for each pair, coming from either the individual's biological father or biological mother. This means that every individual can produce some 8 million different combinations of chromosomes. Therefore a large degree of genetic variation is possible even between siblings.

The unique combination of genes a child receives from her parents via their sperm and ovum is called the **genotype**. Not all of a child's genetic makeup is realized in full. The child's observable traits are known as the **phenotype** and include both physical and psychological characteristics.

Children inherit genes, not behavioral patterns or psychological characteristics, but genetic factors can affect the likelihood of a child developing in a certain way. The term **behavioral phenotype** is used when a specific set of psychological characteristics seems to be linked to a known genetic syndrome or the presence of one or more genes. Only rarely however are children with a particular genetic syndrome or chromosomal anomaly characterized by a specific behavioral pattern (Hodapp, 1997).

Dominant and Recessive Traits

A wide range of traits and conditions are partially or completely determined by genes. This applies to eye color, skin color and so forth. Mendel's laws of inheritance describe how genetically determined

DOI: 10.4324/9781003292456-4

traits vary with the genes inherited from the parent generation. Some of the properties are dominant; others are recessive. A *dominant* trait will always assert itself when the gene is present on one of the chromosomes in a pair. A *recessive* trait must be transferred via both parents, meaning that the gene must be present on both chromosomes in a pair to be expressed. All people are carriers of **recessive genes** and thus ble to pass on the genetic basis of traits they themselves do not have. Examples of dominant traits are brown eyes, curly hair and far-sightedness. Straight hair and normal vision are recessive. The same applies to blue eyes. Because the genetic basis for brown eyes is dominant, parents with completely blue eyes cannot have the gene for brown eyes and are therefore unable to conceive brown-eyed children.

The distribution of dominant and recessive genes can cause siblings to look quite different or differ considerably from each other in other ways. In some cases, a given genetic constellation can lead to serious illness or **disability** in one or more children in a family, while siblings with a different constellation develop normally. If the disease is caused by recessive genes, they can still be carriers, and genetic counselling is usually offered when a child in the family has a disability that may have a genetic basis.

Autosomal and Sex-Linked Inheritance

All chromosomes other than sex chromosomes are *autosomal*. Conditions associated with the genes on these chromosomes occur as frequently in males as in females. When a gene located on a sex chromosome leads to an increased probability of a particular development, it is referred to as **sex-linked inheritance**. Genes located on the Y chromosome only affect the development of boys. As most of the genes on this chromosome are recessive, the majority of recessive genes on the X chromosome of males will be expressed, while the recessive genes on the X chromosome of females will more likely be suppressed by a non-recessive allele on the other X chromosome. This means that conditions linked to the X chromosome are more frequent in males than in females. Twice as many boys as girls are color blind, for example. Sex chromosomes are involved in a number of known syndromes (see Table 3.1).

Mutation

A mutation is a sudden change of genetic code. Mutations are common to all living organisms and usually occur without any detectable reason, but they may increase owing to the influence of X-rays and certain chemical substances, for example. Some mutations lead to changes in gene expression, while others have little impact. Many **chromosomal abnormalities** and genetically determined conditions are caused by mutations. When mutations occur in gametes,

Table 3.1 Some common chromosomal disorders and genetically determined conditions

Angelman syndrome is caused by a genetic defect on chromosome 15 inherited from the mother, the counterpart to Prader-Willi syndrome. Most affected children have severe or profound **intellectual disability** and lack speech. They are hyperactive, inquisitive and often have a happy demeanor. Their movements are stiff and puppet-like. **Prevalence** is estimated at 1 in 15,000

Down syndrome is caused by a partial or complete extra chromosome 21. Common characteristics are a flat neck, slanted eyes, malformations of the outer ear, an increased **incidence** of heart disease and premature aging. This **chromosomal abnormality** is the most common cause of severe intellectual disability and makes up approximately 20 percent of this group of disorders. On average, 1 in 800 children have Down syndrome. The incidence increases with the mother's age at the time of birth

Huntington disease is caused by a **dominant gene** located on chromosome 4. It is a neurodegenerative brain disorder characterized by involuntary jerky movements, particularly involving the face, tongue, neck, shoulders, arms and legs. Speech is often slurred, and eating and swallowing are problematic.

Prader-Willi syndrome is caused by a genetic defect on chromosome 15 inherited from the father (see also Angelman syndrome). Common characteristics are low muscle tone (**hypotonia**), special facial features, small feet, delayed motor and language development and mild or moderate intellectual disability. Children with this syndrome often have problems thriving during their first year of life. Later in life they tend to develop an insatiable appetite and major problems with being overweight. Prevalence is about 1 in 15,000

Rett syndrome is believed to be caused by a defect in a gene on the X chromosome (mostly MeCP$_2$) that prevents some genes on this chromosome from being switched off when they should be (see **genomic imprinting** below). It is uncertain whether the syndrome can affect boys. Girls with Rett syndrome have profound intellectual disability as well as motor and language impairment. Most of them have a normal development during the first 6–18 months of life, and some develop speech. Following this, they experience a decline and lose their speech and other skills. Later development is extremely limited in most areas, but may show some improvement in social functioning. Prevalence is about 1 in 10,000 female births

(Continued)

Table 3.1 (Continued)

Initial symptoms may include changes in personality, impairment of memory, concentration and initiative, and emotional lability. In some cases, the disease appears before the age of 20, but generally symptoms first emerge around the age of 35–45. The prevalence varies from country to country, with an average of 5.7 per 100,000 in studies in Europe, North America and Australia, and significantly fewer in Asian studies

Klinefelter syndrome and *triple X syndrome* (also known as trisomy X) involve the presence of an additional X chromosome. Males with Klinefelter syndrome (XXY) have a feminine distribution of body fat, with long arms and legs and enlarged breast tissue. Females with triple X syndrome (XXX) look normal and often are slightly above medium height. They tend to score somewhat lower than average on intelligence **tests**. An extra X chromosome occurs in about 1 in 1,000 births

Juvenile neuronal ceroid lipofuscinosis (JNCL), also known as **Batten disease**, is an autosomal recessive neurodegenerative disorder. The first symptoms are usually loss of vision at 4–10 years of age. The disease is one of the most common causes of blindness between the ages of 5 and 15. Affected children gradually lose their cognitive, language and motor skills, and nearly all develop epilepsy. Many die in their 20s or earlier, but some can live beyond the age of 30 or even 40 years. Prevalence is about 1 in 30,000

Turner syndrome is caused by a missing X chromosome (X0) in females. The chromosomal abnormality causes the degeneration of ovarian function and a stop in the production of estrogen. Common characteristics are somewhat lower birth weight, heart defect, special facial features, short and broad fingers, a short stature and **learning disorders**. In some adults, hearing is partially impaired. Most of those affected only show some of the characteristics. Prevalence is about 1 in 2,500 female births

Williams syndrome is caused by one or more genes on chromosome 7. Common characteristics are heart defects, special facial features, a short stature, delayed prenatal and later development, difficulties thriving in **infancy** and mild or moderate intellectual disability. Compared with other skills, their language skills tend to be good, and they are social and trusting. Prevalence is estimated at 1 in 7,500

their hereditary properties are changed, while the result of mutations in other cells cannot be inherited.

There is a positive **correlation** between mutations and parental age. For females, and to a lesser extent males, the **risk** of having a child with an extra chromosome in one pair of chromosomes (trisomy) increases with age, including a child with Down syndrome (**trisomy 21**). Males above the age of 35 have a slightly higher risk of new mutations and thus of transferring certain autosomal dominant conditions (Hassold & Sherman, 2000; McIntosh et al., 1995).

Some mutations reduce the cells' ability to survive and carry out their tasks, but mutations can also have a positive impact. They lead to changes in the gene pool and thus a species' ability to evolve. Every human being has an average of 300 mutations.

Genomic Imprinting

According to Mendel's model, it is irrelevant whether a gene comes from the mother or the father. It has been found however that a gene can function differently depending on whether it is maternal or paternal. This is explained by the fact that one of the two alleles in a pair has been *imprinted*. **Imprinting** means that a gene is "silenced" or "switched off" if the child inherits the gene from one parent, but not if the same gene is passed on from the other parent. Both Angelman syndrome and Prader-Willi syndrome are caused by missing genetic material on chromosome 15 (see Table 3.1). Children develop Angelman syndrome when the relevant paternal genes are turned off and the maternal genes remain active, and Prader-Willi syndrome when the maternal genes are switched off and the paternal genes remain active (Davies et al., 2015; Kopsida et al., 2011). Genomic imprinting usually involves not a permanent change or mutation in DNA, but a temporary or permanent change in the *function* of part of an individual's DNA (Choufani & Weksberg, 2016; Swaney, 2011).

The above example of Angelman and Prader-Willi syndromes illustrates genomic imprinting with abnormal development, but usually imprinting involves normal genetic mechanisms. It is a way of regulating the effect of different genes and hence related to epigenesis (see p. 00). So far, approximately 100 imprinted genes have been described (Choufani & Weksberg, 2016). The imprinting mechanism is believed to have played an important role in human evolution, as well as in individual development, especially in regulating prenatal and **postnatal** brain development (Perez et al., 2016). For example, genes that are switched off are activated during specific phases of development. By using the gene from a single parent only, the organism maintains a reserve gene that can be brought into play during periods of rapid growth, or in case of cellular mutations or dysfunctions (Kopsida et al., 2011; Wilkinson et al., 2007). Genomic imprinting shows that the mechanisms underlying the transfer of genetic information from one generation to the next, and the way in which the organism deals with this information, are both complex and flexible.

4

Evolution

Evolution is the process by which different species have developed. According to Charles Darwin's theory of evolution (1859), a species undergoes constant changes over time. Certain genes contribute to properties that enable individuals in a given environment to grow up and reproduce more successfully in that environment than individuals lacking those genes. The prevalence of these genes increases because individuals carrying them generate offspring and spread their genes more than those who do not carry them. Other genes do not lead to the development of traits that result in increased reproduction in a given environment. As these genes are propagated less, their incidence among the **population** declines. As a result of this process, species undergo constant transformation. Given the right conditions, individual differences can also evolve into differences between species. This is known as "**natural selection**," but it is important to emphasize that the process does not create new characteristics or skills, but simply ensures that individuals with certain existing characteristics and skills have a better chance of survival than others. Evolution does not explain *where* new traits and adaptations come from, only *why* they propagate (Gottlieb, 2002).

Evolution thus entails a process of interaction between genes and the environment. Individual differences in genetic makeup are a prerequisite for evolution to take place, and any one environment will promote the spread of certain genes and inhibit that of others. The process is a slow one however. Therefore, from a Darwinian perspective, evolutionary adaptation can only take place when environmental characteristics are stable over many generations. Prior to Darwin, Lamarck (1809) maintained that acquired characteristics can be inherited – dependent on whether they are used or not used – and this view

DOI: 10.4324/9781003292456-5

Charles Darwin

has been brought up in the recent discussion of epigenetic processes (see below), where genetic alterations in gene function are sometimes thought to be transmitted across generations. However, evidence of such transmission is limited, and social inheritance seems a stronger process (Heard & Martienssen, 2014).

5

Gene Regulation, Epigenesis and Development

The information contained in the genes of the very first cell (**zygote**), produced by the union of two germ cells (gametes), is a necessary prerequisite for the formation of an individual organism. The particular genes inherited by a child are determined by the parents' genetic makeup, but an optimal course of development requires environmental characteristics and genetic functioning to be adapted to one another. The individual's genetic structure or code sequence is stable, but the function of the genes, their production of RNA, is adaptable and dynamic. Genes do not exist independently of the environment but represent tendencies to react differently to specific environmental characteristics (Manuck & McCaffery, 2014).

Epigenesis is a process which involves mechanisms that regulate the function of genes without changing their structure, including imprinting (Zhang & Meaney, 2010). It is faster than structural genetic change and hence represents mechanisms for flexibility and adaption to the immediate environment (Heard & Martienssen, 2014). Studies show that the environment can influence gene activity by way of a "calibration" to the environment as it manifests itself through the child's experiences. The process can be compared with the activation of the immune system, which requires appropriate stimulation in order to prepare for the particular bacteria found in a child's environment. The ability to form antibodies is innate, but the specific antibodies developed by the child depend on the bacterial environment. Genes are innate, but it is the epigenetic process that determines how they are expressed. Early experiences prepare the individual for certain environmental conditions, a preparedness that continues throughout life, but the balance between gene function and expression may nevertheless change throughout the entire life cycle, and epigenetic effects may

DOI: 10.4324/9781003292456-6

be reversible (McGowan & Szyf, 2010; Tammen et al., 2013). This emphasizes that gene function is a dynamic developmental process.

The role of the epigenetic process is to ensure **typical development** under different environmental conditions but the process sometimes goes wrong and leads to **atypical development** (Gapp et al., 2014). Brain development and function are particularly targeted by epigenetic influences, and disruption of epigenetic regulation is believed to be involved in profound disorders such as Rett syndrome (Zahir & Brown, 2011) and neurodevelopmental disorders such as **autism spectrum disorder** (Geschwind, 2011; Millan, 2013). Rett syndrome is mainly related to mutation in the regulation gene MeCP2, leading to dysregulation of gene expression and severely disturbed brain development with many cells and few **synapses** (Amir et al., 1999; Ehrhart et al., 2016; Lyst & Bird, 2015).

One of the fundamental questions regarding nature versus nurture is *how* genes function and impact the development of an individual, in other words how the genotype contributes to growth and change and to the formation of a phenotype. For example, it is estimated that several hundred genes have importance for the development of cognitive abilities (Kleefstra et al., 2014). This is not to say that these genes carry a predetermined **IQ** score. Genes produce nothing other than proteins, which in turn affect processes such as the production of nerve cells and cell connections in the brain and thereby affect the ability to solve cognitive problems (Vaillend et al., 2008). One example of this is **phenylketonuria** (PKU), a hereditary defect in the production of one or more enzymes necessary to metabolize an essential amino acid (phenylalanine). Without treatment, affected children suffer neurological damage and severe intellectual disability, but a special diet low in phenylalanine allows them to develop normally (Crusio, 2015). All newborn children are screened for the disease. There is no doubt about the genetic cause of this metabolic disorder, but any damage to cognitive functioning would be the result of both genes and the environment. Although a basic **vulnerability** exists, the diet protects the child from any severe developmental consequences. The effect of genes is not absolute, but may involve an increased or reduced likelihood of a certain development (Rutter, 2006).

The formation of an individual by interaction between genes and environment means that a mechanism, or "meeting point," must exist for genes and experience to influence one another. Internal neurological activity and external stimulation can activate as well as inhibit the function of genes. This can occur when hormones susceptible to the influence of the organism's experiences penetrate the cellular nucleus and trigger gene activity. During very early development, for example, the activity of a number of genes depends on sensory stimulation. The ability of these genes to adjust their own function and that of other genes allows the organism to achieve the same developmental result by making use of different genetic resources (Gottlieb, 2007). In a certain sense, every individual is created anew. In the course of development, the system creates its own genotype by activating and suppressing genes inherited from the parents and improving the proteins being produced (Elman, 2005; Hyde, 2015).

The fact that gene effects are not a one-way road is captured by the development model of Gottlieb (1992, 2007). It consists of four levels, and genetic activity is represented by the lowest level (Figure 5.1). Nerve activity is located between genetic activity and behavior and, in turn, influences both these levels. The connection between nerve activity and behavior forms the neurological basis for carrying out actions and creating mental **representations** of actions. Behavior affects the physical, social and cultural aspects of the environment and is influenced by the latter. Experience based on action and perception affects neurological activity, which in turn affects genetic activity and gene regulation. At any one time, the organism

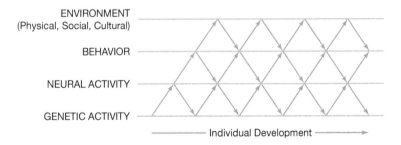

Figure 5.1 Mutual interaction between different levels.

Developmental model consisting of four levels that influence each other: genetic activity, nerve activity, behavior and environment. Behavior includes all forms of human mental activity (motor planning, perception, thinking, problem solving etc.). The environment includes the physical, social and cultural characteristics of the individual's surroundings (based on Gottlieb, 1992, p. 186).

is the result of previous genetic and environmental influences. This corroborates the fact that neither genes nor the environment are sufficient in themselves to ensure development. An organism depends on the functions and **constraints** dictated by its genes and the environmental influences it is able to exploit. The question of genes and the environment is – literally – the question of what came first: the chicken or the egg.

6

Heredity and Environment in Individual Differences

The relationship between the impact of nature and nurture on individual differences in intelligence, personality, social ability and other areas may well be the most basic issue in developmental psychology and is discussed in many places in the complete book. Heredity refers to the genes that are transferred to the child by the mother and father. The physical environment includes all of the chemical and physical influences an individual is exposed to, from conception to death. The social and cultural environment consists of all the people in an individual's life and includes the child's close social relations as well as broader societal contexts and cultural practices. There are two main ways of studying the influence of heredity and the environment on specific aspects of development: family studies and gene studies.

Family Studies

These studies are based on the fact that people related to one another share all or some of the genes that contribute to individual differences, and that children growing up together are exposed to some of the same influences. The assumption is that individuals who share more genes will be more similar if a particular trait is influenced by genes. Family studies include comparisons of **monozygotic (identical) and dizygotic (fraternal) twins**, siblings who grow up together and separately, and children and their biological and/or foster parents. Identical twins come from the same fertilized egg and share identical genetic material (Figure 6.1). They therefore always have the same gender. Fraternal twins share 50 percent of their genes. The same is true of siblings. As children receive their genes from their parents, they are genetically more similar than individuals who are not related.

DOI: 10.4324/9781003292456-7

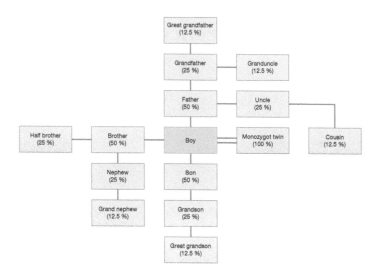

Figure 6.1 Genetic similarities between relatives.

The figure shows the percentage of genetic material shared between a boy and his male relatives. Owing to the nature of sex chromosomes, percentages differ slightly across gender boundaries (based on Plomin et al., 1997, p. 29).

Children of identical twins are half-siblings from a genetic point of view as they genetically have a single parent in common.

Because identical twins share the same gene structure, twin studies have been particularly important in shedding light on the impact of genes and the environment. The similarity between identical twins who have grown up together reflects both their shared inheritance and environment. When identical twins who have grown up separately are less similar, it must be owing to differences in their rearing environments. Assuming that the environments of identical twins growing up apart do not contribute to similarities between them, their similar traits must be caused by their shared genes.

A correlation is an expression of interdependence or agreement between variables (see Book 1, *Theoretical Perspectives and Methodology*, Chapter 24) and may indicate how similar people are with regard to a specific characteristic, such as the IQ of parents and children. Studies have shown that the correlations for height, intelligence, temperament, personality and many other human characteristics increase with the amount of shared genetic material (Table 6.1). There is thus little

Twins can be difficult to distinguish

doubt that genetic inheritance influences the development of many characteristics, but the same is true of the environment. Children with different appearances and abilities are met in different ways and may therefore experience and react to the same environment in dissimilar ways. Identical twins, who physically resemble each other more than fraternal twins, most likely are met more similarly by others, thereby reacting more equally to an environment than fraternal twins. Identical twins create more similar environments for themselves than fraternal twins, even if they grow up apart. On the other hand, epigenetic differences contribute to diversity in gene expression also among twins (Little, 2011). When fraternal twins are more similar to one another than to other siblings, it must be owing to greater similarities in the environment, as they were born at the same time. After all, both fraternal twins and regular siblings share approximately 50 percent of their genes (Spinath et al., 2004).

Family studies show that correlations within pairs of twins and between siblings change in the course of **childhood** and the life cycle (Lenroot & Giedd, 2008). In a **longitudinal study** of nearly 500 pairs of twins, Wilson (1983) found roughly the same correlations between intelligence scores for identical and fraternal twins during early childhood. By the age of 6, the pairs of identical twins had become significantly more similar to one another in intelligence than the fraternal

Table 6.1 Examples of correlations between the characteristics of people with varying degrees of genetic and environmental similarity (correlations vary from study to study)

	Intelligence	Height	Weight	Extroversion	Neuroticism
Identical twins together	0.86	0.93	0.83	0.51	0.46
Identical twins apart	0.76	0.86	0.73	0.38	0.38
Fraternal twins together	0.60	0.66	0.46	0.18	0.20
Fraternal twins apart				0.05	0.23
Siblings	0.47		0.34	0.20	0.20
Adopted siblings	0.32		0.01	0.07	0.11
Biological parents and child(ren) together	0.42		0.26	0.16	0.16
Biological parents and adopted child(ren) apart	0.24		0.23		
Adoptive parents and adopted child(ren)	0.20		0.00	0.01	0.05

	Anxiety	Activity–impulsivity	Aggression	Religiosity	Masculinity/femininity	Heart rate	Blood pressure
Identical twins together	0.59	0.58	0.49	0.51	0.50	0.54	0.70
Identical twins apart				0.49		0.49	0.64
Fraternal twins together	0.18	0.22	0.28		0.33		

pairs, a difference that remained stable until **adolescence**. One possible explanation may be that some genetically determined characteristics do not emerge until the child has reached a certain age. An alternative explanation is that the effects of gene–environment interactions assert themselves more gradually over time, so that the combined effect of genes and the environment creates greater differences between fraternal than between identical twins.

Development does not occur equally in all areas however: in some areas, the similarity between twins increases with age, in others it decreases, especially when twins do not grow up together. For example, the language of identical twins becomes somewhat more dissimilar with age, while that of fraternal twins becomes a little more similar. For certain **personality traits**, the differences between identical twins increase with age, for others they decrease (McCartney et al., 1990; Viken et al., 1994). A possible reason for this may be that monozygotic twins have a "twin **identity**" that leads them to seek out the same types of environments, while siblings who are similar to one another tend to deliberately try to be different.

Adoption studies have also been used to shed light on the influence of nature and nurture. The personality of adopted children correlates weakly with both their adoptive and their biological parents (Plomin et al., 1998). At the same time, studies show that children adopted into families with a high **socioeconomic status** achieve significantly higher average IQ scores than their biological parents (see Book 4, *Cognition, Intelligence and Learning*, Chapter 28). This indicates that the quality of the environment has an impact on intelligence.

In addition to such correlational studies of traits that vary among the general population, the influence of genes and the environment on psychiatric disorders has been studied by looking at their incidence among members of the same family. This is commonly expressed by indicating the degree of *concordance* – the presence of the same condition in different family members. The concordance rate for severe depression, for example, is 40 percent for identical twins and 11 percent for fraternal twins. The concordance among close relatives is 10 percent for major depressive disorder. This means that a child has a 10-percent probability of experiencing major depression if the parents or siblings exhibit such symptoms. Among the population at large, the probability is 3 percent. Consequently, the risk of depression is more than three times greater for those who have family members with severe depression (Plomin et al., 2008). Similarly, language disorders (Bishop, 2003; Kang & Drayna, 2011), learning disorders (Landerl & Moll, 2010) and autism spectrum disorders (Persico & Napolioni, 2013) are often observed in families.

The emergence of specific family characteristics, particularly special talents such as musicality, has also been used as an argument in favor of a genetic basis for such characteristics – the many famous musicians in Johann Sebastian Bach's family have often been cited as an example. It is difficult however to separate genetic conditions from environmental factors in these types of studies. There can be no doubt about the existence of certain biological prerequisites, such as the ability to distinguish between musical pitches, but the influences of musical activities in a family may be just as important for developing an active relationship with music (Howe et al., 1998).

Heritability Estimates

Behavioral genetics attempts to estimate the relative influence of genes and environment on the development of various traits and abilities (Plomin et al., 2013). Calculating a **heritability estimate** is typically based on the difference between the correlations for identical and fraternal twins. Pairs of twins growing up together are shaped by the same environment, but identical twins share twice as many genes as fraternal twins (100 vs. 50 percent). Table 6.1 shows the correlation of intelligence for identical twins (0.86) and fraternal twins (0.60), where 1.00 means full covariation, and 0.00 means no covariation. The difference in correlation is 0.26. Because only half of the genes differ between identical and fraternal twins, the heritability estimate for intelligence based on this table is twice the difference, or 0.52.

Heritability estimates are used in many contexts but have also been criticized for creating an unrealistic picture of the influence of genes and environment (Gottlieb, 1995; Joseph, 2013; Lerner, 2015). This type of use of correlations is only valid if the influences of heredity and environment are made up of independent **main effects** that can be summed numerically (see Book 1, *Theoretical Perspectives and Methodology*, Chapter 6). Most modern developmental theorists argue in favor of *interaction* between genes and the environment. Thus, the effect of the environment will depend on the individual's genes, and heritability will depend on the environment. Based on an interactive model, there is no fixed relationship between heredity and environment for a given trait, and so the genetic and environmental components are not independent (see Book 1, *Theoretical Perspectives and Methodology*, Chapter 6). The rate of heritability will thus depend on variation in the environment. The more genetically alike two individuals are, the greater the influence of the environment on the differences between them. If their genes are exactly alike, such as in the case of identical twins, all of the differences must be caused by environmental factors. The same applies to differences in the environment. The more similar the environments in which twins grow up, the greater the share of differences between them is caused by genes. A uniform environment will therefore yield high heritability estimates. Consequently, heritability estimates reveal as much about the contribution of the environment as that of genes. Calculating heritability estimates for different environments can still reveal useful information about the various environments' ability to realize positive and negative genetic potentials. If a characteristic is found to have major environmental variation in one place and little such variation in another, it may be possible to identify the particular environmental aspects that contribute to the differences in that specific characteristic (Rose, 1997). An understanding of these mechanisms may enable society to promote positive and prevent negative development in children.

Gene Studies of Typical and Atypical Development

The family studies based on the amount of shared genes indicate that some characteristics may have a genetic basis. But they say little about the underlying functions, and the presence of a particular gene variant may be more important than the amount of shared genes. For example, girls with Rett syndrome (see Table 3.1, p. 00), who mostly share a mutation in the MeCP2 gene, are developmentally more similar to each other than to their parents and siblings, even if they share around 50 percent of the genes with them. However, not all girls with the characteristics of the syndrome have the MeCP2 mutation, and some with the mutation do not present with Rett syndrome, suggesting that there may be more than one genetic pathway to this severe disorder (Mari et al., 2005).

The mapping of the human genome in the first part of the twenty-first century led to a search for genes or gene variants (alleles) that are associated with specific functions or disorders. The most common method has been the study of "candidate genes," where individuals with or without a particular trait or disorder are compared with regard to the presence of one or a few genes selected because existing knowledge about their function suggests that they may play a role in the development of the trait or disorder in question. The other method is the genome-wide search where the gene structure of subjects with a particular trait or disorder is compared with that of individuals without this trait or disorder. Many researchers aim to establish "functional genomics," that is, an overview of the functional consequences of DNA variation (Hudziak & Faraone, 2010). However, it has been difficult to document direct effects of individual genes, and many initial findings have not stood the test of replication and are likely to be chance findings (Faraone et al., 2008; Latham & Wilson, 2010).

Studies have still contributed to new knowledge about how alleles of individual genes can influence development, for example the MAOA gene (Figure 6.2). Children with a low-activity allele of MAOA seem to be more sensitive to social rejection than children with other alleles of the gene (Kim-Cohen et al., 2006). They show a *greater* degree of behavioral problems, **mental disorders** and ADHD after having experienced neglect or physical abuse than children with other alleles of the gene. Under positive rearing conditions, however, they show *fewer* such problems (Caspi et al., 2002; Foley et al., 2004). Another example is the short allele of the 5-HTT gene, which also seems to entail a greater *susceptibility* to the influence of both good and bad environments than the long allele. Under unfavorable environmental conditions, children with a short variant develop more poorly than children with a long variant. Here, the short allele appears to represent vulnerability, and the long allele *resilience* (see Book 1, *Theoretical Perspectives and Methodology*, Chapter 8). Under potentially favorable rearing conditions, however, children with the short allele cope *better* than children with the long allele. In this case, the latter seem to be "vulnerable" in the sense that their development does not reflect their favorable environmental conditions. Therefore, none of the alleles can be said to represent vulnerability, as has often been suggested, but rather susceptibility – children with certain alleles are more susceptible to environmental influences in a particular **domain** than children with other alleles. Long alleles cannot be described as "resilience alleles" either, as they result in poorer development than the short alleles under favorable rearing conditions (Belsky et al., 2009; Pluess & Belsky, 2010). The findings thus suggest that children with a "susceptibility allele" of a gene are more dependent on favorable and relevant

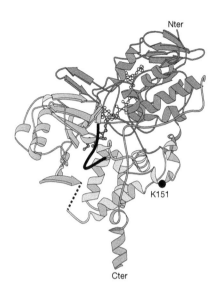

Figure 6.2 Monoamine oxidase A, MAOA, breaks down dopamine, norepineph-
rine and serotonin. (Photo from de Colibus et al., 2005)

environmental conditions than children with other alleles of the gene.
These studies demonstrate that development cannot solely be predicted based on knowledge of the child's genes or on the properties of
the environment. Genes and environment always interact: the same
gene can contribute negatively as well as positively, depending on the
type of environment a child grows up in.

Many disorders have a genetic basis, but there are no specific "intellectual disability genes," "language disorder genes," "autism genes" or
"**dyslexia** genes." They are **developmental disorders**, not "natural" categories with corresponding genes, and many genes seem to be
relevant for several disorders. More than 500 genes have been linked
to intellectual disability (Kleefstra et al., 2014), and several genetic
disruptions and mutations have been linked to language disorders and
other disorders (Bishop, 2003; Kang & Drayna, 2011). Autism spectrum disorders have, over time, been linked to a large number of different genes. Some of these findings are likely to be chance findings
that are not replicable, but they may also reflect that different genes
may influence the development and severity of autism spectrum disorder (Bishop et al., 2014; Persico & Napolioni, 2013).

> To date, hundreds of genetic variants have been associated with ASD, and hundreds of "autism alleles" have been identified, with data on each available on a variety of autism genetic databases.
>
> Bishop et al. (2014, p. 1716)

How genes may function in the neurological development of disorders is illustrated by the studies of an English family that was characterized by language disorders and a disruption of the FOXP2 gene (see Box 6.1). The same gene was found only rarely in children with language disorders, thus demonstrating that different genes may be involved in such disorders. Moreover, the English family had problems not only with language but with all actions that required a sequential organization. It is likely that the gene influenced their ability to construct spoken sentences because the ability to organize sequences of actions is *relevant* for the **language function**, in the same way as it is relevant for the organization of other action sequences in humans and other species (Karmiloff-Smith, 2011). Overall, the studies seem to indicate that several genes may be relevant for the same pathological process, for example autism spectrum disorder or language disorder, and that the same gene may be relevant for different developmental disorders (Bishop et al., 2014).

Similarly, there is no specific personality gene: "Personality is heritable, but it has no genetic mechanism" (Turkheimer et al., 2014, p. 535), and, with the exception of a few rare diseases, there is no direct relationship between individual genes and specific mental disorders (Abdolmaleky et al., 2005). It is more likely that a gene affects general brain properties, such as the ability to regulate emotional arousal, and that these properties can manifest themselves in different ways, depending on the child's other traits and the environment. Heritability estimates for **antisocial behavior**, for example, have been found to lie between 0.3 and 0.4. Relevant genes do not specify such behavior; they can influence traits such as temperament, activity level or attention, factors that in turn represent a vulnerability to developing antisocial behavior (Rutter, 2006).

Some variants of genes (alleles) are more prominent in certain geographic areas than in others, leading researchers to speculate about a

Box 6.1 The FOXP2 Gene and Verbal Apraxia

In an English family, 15 of 37 members had a severe form of verbal **dyspraxia**, problems performing the speech movement, and also many grammatical problems. A genome-wide search found that the family had a disruption of the FOXP2 gene on chromosome 7 (Lai et al., 2001). The finding led to the assumption that the FOXP2 gene was generally responsible for variation in language competence (Pinker & Jackendoff, 2005), but studies did not find the same mutation in other children with language disorders (Newbury et al., 2002). Further studies revealed that the FOXP2 gene was related not only to language but to the organization of action sequences in general. The English family had problems not only with speech but all actions that required a sequential organization (Karmiloff-Smith, 2011).

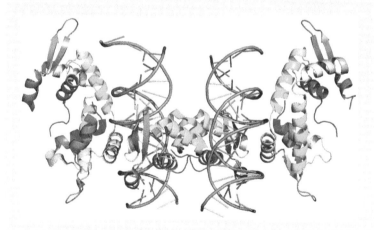

Ill 6.2 Structure of the FOXP2 protein. Based on PyMOL rendering of PDB 2ao9. https://en.wikipedia.org/wiki/FOXP2#/media/
File:Protein_FOXP2_PDB_2a07.png. CC BY-SA 3.0

possible relationship between genes and **culture**. It is common to distinguish between **collectivist** and **individualist cultures**. Studies have found that the short allele of MAOA, which seems to entail greater sensitivity to the social environment, is more frequent in collectivist than in individualist cultures. However, it is impossible to say whether collectivism has evolved as the result of the population's genes or whether individuals with this allele have reproduced more frequently in this type of society (Way & Lieberman, 2010).

It is important to emphasize that most research in this area is cutting-edge, and that knowledge of gene functions remains limited. The results are not unequivocal, and they include both inconsistent and contradictory findings. Studies in different countries, for example, have found apparently contradictory relationships between genes and the characteristics and behavior of children with short and long 5-HTT alleles. Furthermore, the differences in behavior between groups with different alleles are relatively small, and the relationships between behavior and genes are often less pronounced than those between behavior and culture, class, ethnicity or gender (Kagan, 2009). Genes are important, but many factors contribute to an individual's development. Geschwind and Flint (2015) suggest that emotional and **behavioral disorders** are so complex that the search for genes may give limited results, and that more attention should be given to investigating environmental risk factors.

7

Genes and Development: Constraints and Plasticity

It is the species' genes that enable a human sperm cell and ovum to become a human being, and corresponding cells from dogs to become a dog. Genes must constrain the possibilities in such a way that certain developmental outcomes are likely or unavoidable (Keil, 1990). Therefore, the process initiated by the first cell in the fetal environment is guided by strict criteria and constraints. As described earlier, an individual's genes rarely determine a specific developmental result. Cells do not divide and specialize according to a fixed pattern determined at the moment of conception through the unique set of genes passed on from the parents. The genetic architecture allows for sufficient flexibility to make survival possible when the environment changes. It allows room for more developmental possibilities, or **plasticity**. Instead of discussing the effects of heredity and environment, it has become more common to use the terms genetic and environmental constraint and plasticity. The question of nature and nurture, or **maturation** and **learning**, is thus reformulated into a question about constraints in children's potential traits and their plasticity and adaptability.

In discussing the functions of genes, it is important to distinguish between the importance of genes for developing a general trait and the degree to which genes contribute to the differences between individuals. In some domains the constraints are quite strict, with little room for variation. This applies to processes that ensure that nearly all human beings have two eyes, two feet with five toes each and so on. The design of details, on the other hand, has fewer constraints. There is considerable variation in head circumference, eye color, height, appearance, and so on. The greatest differences are in areas with a basis in neurological development, such as cognitive and social skills

DOI: 10.4324/9781003292456-8

and personality. This means that the constraints on brain development are smaller and plasticity is greater than in other areas of growth. It is precisely such characteristics related to neurological function that cause the greatest disagreement from a biological point of view. Here, theories of general plasticity confront theories about genetically specified constraints. An intermediate position is that the brain's general structure and function are subject to strict constraints, while there is considerable plasticity within these constraints (Gottlieb et al., 2006; Johnson et al., 2002).

Behaviorism is located at one end of the scale in regard to nature versus nurture (see Book 1, *Theoretical Perspectives and Methodology*, Chapter 12). Although the significance of genes for the development of the human organic structure is acknowledged, including the design of the brain, evolutionary selection is assumed to have provided neurological plasticity of such a magnitude that it does not imply any restrictions on behavioral development. As, biologically speaking, plasticity is shared by all human beings, any variation in behavior must be caused by environmental differences, and thus learning.

At the other end of the scale lies the theoretical possibility that developmental changes are the result of genetically determined constraints and maturation, and that the primary function of the environment is to trigger innate knowledge. This means that the dissimilarities between children are solely due to differences in genetic makeup. **Nativism** is located at this end of the scale, but most theoreticians do not consider the constraints to be so strict as to assign no importance to the environment (see Book 1, *Theoretical Perspectives and Methodology*, Chapter 15).

Nonetheless, some theorists ascribe nearly all importance to genes under normal development. According to Scarr (1992, 1996), genes contribute, substantially and directly, not only to development but also to children's experiences: "genotypes drive experience" (1992, p. 9). By this she means that genes provide children with traits that lead them to seek out special experiences and thereby form their own environment. Assuming that a child grows up in an "average expected environment," including what Scarr calls a "normal home environment," parents will merely provide the environment that children themselves seek out based on their genetic dispositions. Consequently, the only function of the environment is to realize the child's genetic predisposition, and it does not in and of itself contribute to the differences between children. It is principally the genetic basis that determines the developmental process, a process that, according to Scarr, is difficult to modify. Only when the environment differs dramatically from the norm and is "really deprived, abusive, and neglectful" does Scarr (1992, p. 3) believe it may be able to affect children negatively. She also believes that learning is most constrained early in life, and that plasticity increases with age because children are freer in their choice of environment.

Baumrind (1993) criticizes Scarr's one-sided emphasis on genes as the cause of individual differences. According to Scarr's model, children are passive agents for their genes, both in regard to intelligence and personality. It is the environment, not the individual, that is being adapted. Scarr's view furthermore implies that the differences between human races are mainly caused by variations in their genetic makeup, and only in extreme cases by different rearing conditions and cultural factors. This means that any attempt to improve the development of children growing up in a "normal" environment will have no effect, a view that is not supported by research (Baumrind et al., 2010; Flynn, 2016).

Most developmental psychologists position themselves between radical behaviorism and strong nativism, with major variations in the emphasis they place on genes versus the environment. In areas such as language, personality and intelligence, the theoretical differences are especially pronounced (see elsewhere in this book for discussions of these). Additionally, many theorists question the very notion of separating the effects of genes from those of the environment.

Summary of Part I

1   *Genes* are an essential biological component in human functioning. How human genes have evolved through evolution (phylogeny) and how they contribute to the physical, perceptual, cognitive and social development of human beings (ontogeny) are key questions in developmental psychology.

2   With the exception of reproductive cells (gametes), every human cell normally contains *23 pairs of chromosomes* with a total of approximately 23,000 different genes. Each gene can have several *alleles*.

3   *Genetic inheritance* refers to the information transmitted to a human being or animal via the genes contained in the parents' sperm and egg cell. A child's complete genetic material is called the *genotype*; its observable characteristics are called the *phenotype*. In order for *recessive genes* to affect development, children must inherit them from both parents. If a gene is *dominant*, it only needs to be transmitted by one of the parents in order to be expressed. A *mutation* is a sudden change in a gene structure.

4   *Genomic imprinting* means that a gene can be "switched off," and that the function of the gene depends on which parent it comes from. Genomic imprinting has an important function in regulating brain development.

5   Genes affect processes on other levels and are in turn affected by those processes. The genetic information inside the cells thus constantly interacts with what has previously been established via development and environmental influences. Plasticity is greatest in areas related to neurological function and development.

6   Genes affect and are in turn affected by other genes, as well as by external factors. *Epigenesis* refers to experience-driven changes in

gene function without changes in gene structure. Gene expression seems to be "calibrated" early on, creating a preparedness that continues throughout life, but requires specific environmental conditions in order to be realized.

7 The influence of heredity and the environment on specific aspects of development are investigated with family studies and gene studies. Studies of twins, siblings and other biological and adopted family members show a complex interaction between genetic predisposition and environment in the development of *individual traits*. *Heritability estimates* are based on the difference in correlation between identical (monozygotic) and fraternal (dizygotic) twins. They indicate the relative importance of genes for various traits, but there is disagreement about the usefulness of such estimates.

8 Studies of *candidate genes* compare individuals with or without a particular trait or disorder with regard to the presence of one or a few genes. In a *genome-wide search*, the gene structure of subjects with a particular trait or disorder is compared with that of individuals without this trait or disorder.

9 There is rarely a direct effect of a gene on human traits and disorders. Some studies have found that certain alleles of MAOA, 5-HTT and other genes cause an increased susceptibility to environmental influences, but many of the findings are inconsistent and contradictory. The behavioral differences between individuals with different alleles of a gene are often smaller than the differences caused by culture, class, ethnicity or gender.

10 Development is a balance between constraint and plasticity. Behaviorists maintain that development is plastic and the development of individual differences mainly a result of learning, whereas nativists believe that such differences are largely the result of genetic constraints and maturation. Other theorists believe development to be the result of interaction between genes and the environment, but vary in their emphasis on nature and nurture.

Core Issues

• The relationship between nature and nurture in development.
• What methods to use to measure the influence of genes and environment.

Suggestions for Further Reading

Geschwind, D. H. (2011). Genetics of autism spectrum disorders. *Trends in Cognitive Sciences, 15*, 409–416.

Gottlieb, G. (1995). Some conceptual deficiencies in "developmental" behavior genetics. *Human Development, 38*, 131–141.

Lerner, R. M. (2015). Eliminating genetic reductionism from developmental science. *Research in Human Development, 12*, 178–188.

Plomin, R., DeFries, J. C., Knopik, V. S., & Neiderhiser, J. M. (2016). Top 10 replicated findings from behavioral genetics. *Perspectives on Psychological Science, 11*, 3–23.

Zhang, T. Y., & Meaney, M. J. (2010). Epigenetics and the environmental regulation of the genome and its function. *Annual Review of Psychology, 61*, 439–466.

Part II

Stimulation and Activity during Fetal Development

8

Fetal Development

Development begins at conception when an egg and a sperm cell unite in a single cell. From here until birth, the fetus develops many characteristics and abilities, all made possible by the fetal environment – it protects the immature organism from injury and sensory stimuli the fetus cannot cope with and facilitates stimulation and movement that prepare the organism for an independent life. A key question is how physiological and other factors during fetal development contribute to the differences between children. Although technical developments have opened up new possibilities, the opportunities for studying children in the womb are extremely limited, and both studies and possible interventions pose significant methodological challenges and ethical dilemmas.

Fetal development can be divided into three periods. *The germ* is the seed, the early embryo, and the **germinal period** includes the first 10 days of development. The egg and the sperm merge into a single cell and develop into 60 cells during the first 4 days. After a few days, the cells begin to cluster together into three layers. The outer layer (ectoderm) develops into the skin and nervous system. The middle layer (mesoderm) becomes the skeleton and muscles, while the inner layer (endoderm) evolves into the internal organs (Finne et al., 2001). During the first 8 weeks of development, the fetus is called an *embryo*. The 6-week period following the germinal period is the **embryonic period**, while the **fetal period** lasts until birth.

During the germinal period, all cells are identical and begin to specialize and form different organs during the embryonic period. The middle layer forms the heart, which begins to beat after 3–4 weeks. At 2–3 weeks, the outer layer forms a neural tube, but the nervous system does not begin to develop until the heart has started functioning. By 8 weeks, the fetus has grown to around 2 centimeters in

DOI: 10.4324/9781003292456-10

length and weighs 1 gram. The beginning features of a human being become visible, including the limbs, nervous system and internal organs. At 12 weeks of age, the fetus is about 10 centimeters long and weighs 20 grams. Its human features can be clearly seen. At 20 weeks, its length is about 25 centimeters, and it weighs approximately 300 grams (see Figure 8.1). After that, the weight of the fetus increases significantly, on average from about 1,000 grams to 3,600 grams during the final 3 months. Because the brain is given priority during the fetal period, the size of the head is relatively large compared with the rest of the body. This also applies throughout childhood, and the head does not reach its final proportion in relation to the body until adulthood.

Birth usually occurs after about 40 weeks, and many functions are in place well before the child is born. Circulation is in place after 12 weeks. After 24 weeks, the fetus can breathe in air, but continues to rely on oxygen from the mother's blood because the lungs are still too immature to take up enough oxygen by breathing. Even children born more than 2–3 months prior to term and weighing very little at birth – under 1 kilogram – can survive with medical help but may have to be placed in an incubator.

There is enormous development in the fetal period

The Biochemical Environment

It is the physiological environment that affects the development of the fetus in the womb. The fetus receives nourishment from the mother, whose nutrition and general health affect the fetus's uptake of nutrients and opportunities for growth. An appropriate and balanced diet increases the likelihood of pregnancy without complications, while malnutrition and deficiencies increase the risk of miscarriages, stillbirths and abnormalities. Malnutrition can affect the growth of brain cells, but may to some extent be counteracted if the child receives proper nutrition after birth (Fifer et al., 2004; Hales & Barker, 2001).

Maternal diseases can affect the development of the fetus. Maternal diabetes may reduce growth and delay development, and it is therefore important to regulate the mother's glucose level during pregnancy (Mulder & Visser, 2016). Rubella can cause sensory impairment and other developmental disorders in the child during the first 3 months of pregnancy, in some cases also later. Because of the potentially serious consequences of the disease, girls in many countries are vaccinated against rubella (De Santis et al., 2006).

Substances that can harm the fetus are called **teratogens**. Children whose mothers smoke weigh less at birth, probably because nicotine causes the blood vessels in the uterus to contract and reduce the supply of nutrients. Maternal smoking during pregnancy also increases the risk of congenital heart conditions, premature birth and stillbirth, often in combination with other risk factors (Cnattingius, 2004; Mund et al., 2013).

Drinking relatively large quantities of alcohol during pregnancy leads to a greater risk of birth defects and developmental injuries in the child (Hepper, 2016; O'Leary & Bower, 2012). Particularly in the early stages of pregnancy, alcohol affects the development of the child's brain, often together with smoking and poor nutrition. The brain becomes smaller, and the **cortex** develops fewer folds than normal (Guerrini et al., 2007). There is a relationship between the mother's alcohol consumption and later **hyperactivity** in the child. If the mother has consumed a lot of alcohol over time during pregnancy, the child may develop **fetal alcohol syndrome**, characterized by a small head, characteristic facial features and abnormalities of the heart and limbs. Additionally, children with this syndrome are often irritable and hyperactive (Riley et al., 2011).

Some children are exposed to other substances such as cocaine and heroin during the fetal period. As newborns they may show withdrawal symptoms that include tremors, hypersensitivity, problems focusing the eyes and self-regulating, crying and sleeping problems. The symptoms eventually disappear but can make the child's early interactions with adults difficult. Cocaine causes the mother's blood vessels to constrict and deprives the fetus of nutrition. Prolonged use increases the risk of delayed development, but the results of studies

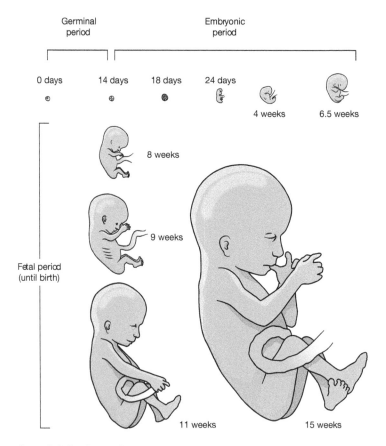

Figure 8.1 Fetal growth.

Changes in the relative size and shape of a fetus until 15 weeks of age (based on Butterworth & Harris, 1994, p. 38).

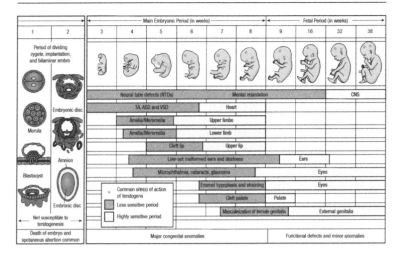

Figure 8.2 Sensitivity to damage from toxins during fetal development.

Different organs and parts of the body are vulnerable at various times during fetal development. The figure shows periods in which particular parts of the fetus are especially sensitive, somewhat sensitive and not sensitive to the influence of teratogenic agents such as nicotine, alcohol, drugs and various medications. Generally, the risk of major defects is greatest during the embryonic period. The figure also shows the effects of teratogens on other features at different stages of pregnancy (Moore & Persaud, 2008, p. 473).

on the long-term effects on **cognition**, language and behavior vary. Children who have been exposed to heroin during the fetal period have problems with attention and perceptual and cognitive functioning in childhood, even if taken away from the mother and placed in a sound and nurturing environment. Boys are more vulnerable than girls (Behnke et al., 2013; Irner, 2012). Variations in the results most likely reflect differences in exposure and in the quality of follow-up care given to mothers and children.

The effects of various substances on fetal development depend on when and for how long the fetus has been exposed to them. Different organs and parts of the body are vulnerable at different times (see Figure 8.2). Harmful exposure to teratogens for example tends to lead to heart failure early in the germinal period, while the brain is the organ most at risk during the final part of prenatal development. The effects of malnutrition and maternal smoking are greatest during the last 5 months, when the fetus increases most in weight.

Exposure to alcohol and drugs during fetal development also implies an increased vulnerability to environmental risk factors. This means that negative environmental factors can lead to more severe developmental consequences for children exposed to such substances than for other children (Yumoto et al., 2008).

9

Prenatal Stimulation

Perceptual and cognitive development begins with the fetal period. The cells divide and form a brain that is able to perceive, process and remember sensory information and create simple patterns of movement. Sensory stimulation activates the nervous system and thereby fulfills an important function in neurological development. The development of the senses occurs in a fixed order: first the tactile sense and the sense of balance, followed by smell and taste, then hearing, and finally vision. All of these have begun to function before the fetus is 26 weeks old (Lecanuet & Schaal, 2002). This temporal sequence prevents competition between the different sensory systems and facilitates their organization and **integration** (Turkewitz & Kenny, 1985).

The senses receive different types of stimulation during fetal development. The balance system is stimulated by the mother's movements, and her physical activity may cause pressure or vibration on the fetus (Ronca & Alberts, 1995). At 10–11 weeks, the fetus responds to *tactile stimulation* of the hands and arms and, after 14 weeks, it responds to touch all over its body, except for the top of the head. The most common responses in studies of fetal development are changes in heart rate and amount of body movement (see Reissland & Kisilevsky, 2016). The neurological structures and chemical substances necessary to perceive *pain* are activated late in fetal life, although it is uncertain whether fetuses can feel pain (Piontelli et al., 2015). Moreover, the fetal environment includes little "acute" stimulation that could be painful (Hepper, 1992).

Over time, the fetus is able to perceive different chemical substances as precursors to *odor* and *taste*. A fetus swallows more amniotic fluid when a sweetener has been added than when the fluid is neutral or when a bitter-tasting substance has been added (Schaal et al., 1995).

DOI: 10.4324/9781003292456-11

The light that reaches the fetus is uniform and extremely weak and provides little basis for visual learning. It is possible that the faint gleam of light that appears during late gestation helps to activate the optic nerves.

The fetus is exposed to a relatively high degree of acoustic stimulation from the mother's internal organs (60–85 dB), but the heartbeat and other sounds lie at a frequency range too low for the fetus to perceive. Other sounds in the child's environment are quite weak (8–32 dB) against the background noise. The child can react to outside sounds, but these must penetrate several layers of tissue and fluids and lose much of their energy in the transition from air to tissue. The liquid that fills the fetus's ears results in a distortion of sounds compared with how similar sounds are perceived after birth (Lecanuet & Schaal, 2002; Querleu et al., 1988). This means that the possibilities of a fetus gaining knowledge about the sounds it will meet in its surroundings after birth are generally poor during the time in the womb.

The mother's voice is a prominent sound in the fetal environment; it has the advantage of being transmitted through the body and can lie as much as 32 dB above other background sounds (Hepper, 1992). Right before term, the fetus will react to the mother's voice with changes in heart rate, a form of attention response (Voegtline et al., 2013). A number of **experiments** using conditioning and habituation have found that newborns are more attentive to their mother's voice than other female voices (see Book 3, *Perceptual and Motor Development*, Chapter 4). This means that the fetus is able to perceive and remember some aspects of the mother's voice. In a study where the mother's speech was presented on tape, the fetus showed the same pattern of response when it was played forward and backward, indicating that the fetus is less attentive to temporal than non-temporal aspects of sounds, such as pitch, frequency and tone (Kisilevsky, 2016). Reduced fetal growth may be associated with delayed auditory development. Newborns who are small for gestational age more frequently fail to show preference for their mother's voice and score significantly lower on **expressive language** measures at 15 months (Kisilevsky et al., 2014).

The fetus reacts to sounds (or vibration) at 12–16 weeks of age, *before* the development of hearing. This suggests that the fetus experiences a form of *general* sensory stimulation that cannot be compared to hearing. Studies of visual perception performed during the first months after birth also show that newborn babies (and thus the fetus) perceive visual stimulation differently than infants only a few months of age (see Book 3, *Perceptual and Motor Development*, Chapter 3).

The reactions to stimulation change in the course of fetal development. For example, early on, contact with the cheek will cause the fetus to withdraw from the source of stimulation. Later on, the fetus will turn toward the source of contact. This may be in preparation for the **rooting reflex**, which, after birth, helps children find their mother's nipple with their mouth in order to suck (see Book 3, *Perceptual and Motor Development*, Chapter 8). Stimulation of the senses contributes to the development of fetal movements and aids in the transition from the womb to the outside environment (Hepper, 1992; Ronca & Alberts, 1995). Hence, the function of fetal perception is not to remember certain experiences but to prepare for the different types of stimulation the child will meet after birth. As the amount of amniotic fluid decreases toward the end of pregnancy, the fetus receives progressively more stimulation (Ronca & Alberts, 1995). Prematurely born babies are developmentally adapted to the protected fetal environment and have a limited ability to deal with stimulation from their surroundings and so they need help to shield themselves against overstimulation (McMahon et al., 2012; Yecco, 1993).

Movement and Activity

With a length of 2–3 centimeters, the fetus begins to move by curling up and stretching out after about 7 weeks. After another 3–4 weeks, it begins to roll, turn its head and move individual limbs. After 16 weeks, the movements are so distinct that mothers begin to notice them. The grasping **reflex** shows up after 28 weeks.

Fetuses generally move a lot, especially in the early fetal stage. At 16 weeks, a fetus makes up to 20,000 movements per day. Ultrasound studies have shown that *inactivity* increases with age, a phenomenon thought to be caused by the fact that higher parts of the brain assume motor control. Prior to week 24, the fetus never rests for more than 5 minutes at a time. At 32 weeks, most inactive periods last between 10 and 35 minutes and only rarely more than 40 minutes (Pillai & James, 1990). The fetus also has a 96-minute wake–sleep cycle that is associated with the mother's own sleeping patterns and disappears after birth (de Vries et al., 1982, 1985, 1988).

The activity of the fetus strengthens its body, develops its senses, provides feedback about its physical growth and forms the basis for the development of behavior the child shows at birth. Fewer movements are associated with reduced mobility in the joints, growth disorders and malformations in the lungs and face (Ronca & Alberts, 1995). Children with *fetal alcohol syndrome* have abnormalities in the joints believed to be the result of sedation of the fetus by alcohol in the mother's blood, leading to reduced motor activity during a sensitive period in the development of the joints (Butterworth & Harris, 1994).

Initially, movement is *spontaneous*, that is, not caused by any external influence. Gradually, movement is progressively triggered by sensory stimulation. When the fetus is 20–27 weeks old, loud noises and vibrations begin to cause changes in the heart rate (Joseph, 2000). After 33 weeks, the fetus reacts with large movements when stimulated by sound (Gagnon, 1992), although the reaction time is quite slow: an increase in movement first occurs 10 minutes after stimulation and lasts for 1 hour. This delayed reaction most likely indicates that the fetus needs time to process stimulation.

Similar to studies conducted on sensory stimulation, research has found skills that are not easily detected in the fetal environment and will prove to be important in the external environment after birth. This emphasizes the fact that fetal development is about more than physical growth, and that it takes time for a child to develop the perceptual and motor skills shown by newborn children.

Prenatal Learning

Prenatal learning – defined as a change in behavior (for example heart rate) as a direct result of experience – can entail habituation, conditioning and exposure. Most research has been conducted on animal fetuses (James, 2010). In humans, the onset of habituation – usually a decrease in reaction following repeated stimulation (see Book 1, *Theoretical Perspectives and Methodology*, Chapter 25), for example an electric toothbrush placed on the maternal abdomen over the fetal head and activated in 5-second periods approximately every 20 seconds – appears to become established at roughly the same time as the senses begin to function, around weeks 25–28, and somewhat earlier in girls than in boys (Leader, 2016). Prenatal habituation requires a stimulus to be presented many times before the reaction becomes substantially reduced, but the number declines with age (McCorry & Hepper, 2007).

Towards the end of the **prenatal period**, the fetus also shows a capacity for **long-term memory** in connection with stimulation. In one study, the same auditory stimulus was repeated until the reactions of the fetus had decreased (habituation). When the experiment was repeated the following day, fewer iterations were needed to establish a corresponding degree of habituation. When the repetition took place after 3 days, no such learning effect was observable (Leader, 1995), indicating that the limit of fetal memory is more than 1 day and less than 3 days (see also Book 4, *Cognition, Intelligence and Learning*, Chapter 10).

The **association** between a stimulus and a response (see Book 4, *Cognition, Intelligence and Learning*, Chapter 35) is mainly based on animal studies using **classical conditioning**, and little research has been conducted on human fetuses. Although some studies have found evidence of this type of learning, others have not. Therefore, it remains uncertain whether the human fetus is sufficiently developed for this type of learning (James, 2010).

10

Fetal Experiences and Later Development

As the fetal period forms the basis for further development, it is assumed that the course of fetal development has a certain bearing on the child's future development. Also, the fetus adapts to its environment, for example by reducing growth when nourishment is sparse (Gluckman & Hanson, 2010; Wells, 2007). This is sometimes referred to as "fetal programming" and includes *epigenetic* influences, the influence of environmental conditions on the expression of genes (Ellison, 2010; Monk et al., 2012; see also Chapter 5, this volume). For example, there is a correlation between fetal reactions to stimulation (measured by changes in the heart rate) and temperament during infancy (Werner et al., 2007). **Continuity** in development is also indicated by heart rate habituation before delivery and later cognitive development (Box 10.1). Similarly, children who are active in the womb tend to continue to be active after birth. It has also been suggested that some neurodevelopmental disorders may have their origin in prenatal processes (van den Bergh, 2011). The prenatal environment may thus have a lasting effect on development.

Another question is the extent to which a fetus can have specific experiences that are stored in memory and can be confirmed after birth. Studies have shown that fetal exposure to chemical substances can affect the child's taste preferences during the **neonatal period**. A fetus that is more attentive to its mother's voice than the voices of strangers right before birth (and after) indicates some kind of memory of the maternal voice (Kisilevsky et al., 2009). This type of **recognition** may increase the likelihood of newborns paying attention to their mother. After all, it is the voice – along with the sense of smell – that forms the basis for the child's initial recognition (Hepper, 2015). It has been speculated that the mother's voice serves as a kind of preparation for the child's attachment, just as

DOI: 10.4324/9781003292456-12

Box 10.1 Habituation and Later Development (Leader, 2016)

The study group consisted of 100 subjects who were tested for habituation with vibro-acoustic stimulation (a vibrator placed above the fetus on the mother's abdomen) 2 weeks before their delivery. Fifty-four of the mothers had uncomplicated pregnancies, and 46 had pregnancies complicated by hypertension intrauterine growth retardation or developed fetal distress in labor. The mean heart rate for 5 seconds before the stimulation was compared with the maximum heart rate achieved in the next 55 seconds. If the fetus did not increase its heart rate by more than ten beats per minute for five successive trials, it was regarded as habituation. The maximum number of trials to meet the habituation criterion was 50. Each fetus was classified as either a habituator or a non-habituator. At 3 years of age, 61 of the children were tested with the Bayley Scales of Infant Development (1993) by a developmental psychologist who was unaware of their earlier status as habituator or non-habituator. The average of both groups were within the normal range, but the habituators had significantly higher scores than the non-habituators on (a) the Mental Developmental Index and (b) the Psychomotor Developmental Index. More of the non-habituators had scores 1 **standard deviation** below the mean or lower (below IQ 85). Similar differences were found at 7–8 years for a subgroup of 32 children, but the results were less consistent and more pronounced for girls than for boys. The results show developmental continuation from fetal life into childhood.

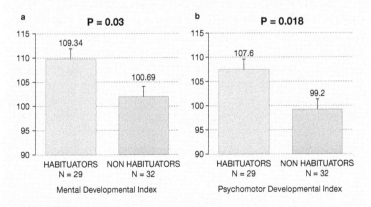

a P = 0.03 — Mental Developmental Index. HABITUATORS N = 29: 109.34; NON HABITUATORS N = 32: 100.69.

b P = 0.018 — Psychomotor Developmental Index. HABITUATORS N = 29: 107.6; NON HABITUATORS N = 32: 99.2.

> Throughout gestation, the mother and her offspring are exquisitely intertwined, forming an integrated, biological system within which the mother, gestating siblings, and fetus itself each contribute in significant and meaningful ways to the fetus's sensory milieu.
>
> (Ronca & Alberts, 2016, p. 21)

the sounds of brooding birds seem to prepare for imprinting (see Book 7, *Social Relations, Self-awareness and Identity*, Chapter 2). No research has been able to show whether this type of prenatal "preparation" affects the attachment process. However, studies show that the mother to some extent bonds with her child during pregnancy. Being able to see the fetus via ultrasound aids in this process (Alhusen, 2008; DiPietro, 2010).

Studies have also found that newborns showed a preference for the music of TV series their mothers had watched during pregnancy, but this disappeared after 3 weeks (Hepper, 1992). Thus, any early recognition of this type is short-lasting, and there is no reason to believe that it is possible to "imprint" children to like certain types of music by exposing them to it during the fetal stage. Nor is there evidence to suggest that additional auditory stimulation during the fetal period has any developmental benefits (James, 2010).

Children show a significant development in perceptual and cognitive functioning during the first months after birth. With the exception of the effect of teratogens, it is not known to what extent stimulation and experiences in the fetal period have significance beyond the general developmental stimulation brought about by activation. Correlations between fetal performance and later functioning indicate some degree of continuity, but the factors influencing fetal performance are not always known. Therefore, one should be cautious in attributing a substantial impact of presumed specific experiences during fetal development on a child's subsequent cognitive and linguistic development. On the whole, the fetal environment is characterized by repetitive and relatively non-specific types of stimulation.

Maternal Emotional States

There has been considerable discussion about the extent to which the mother's emotional state affects the fetal environment and influences the child's later development. When the mother experiences strong fear or anger, her autonomic nervous system is activated. Blood flows to the organs that are important for her defense, such as the brain, heart and muscles, while the blood supply to other parts of the body, including the uterus, decreases. If this state persists over time, it can deprive the fetus of needed nutrition. The fetus may respond with an increase in heart rate and a reduction in activity, a response that is interpreted as an attention reaction resulting from changes in the fetal environment, but there is no direct connection between the mother's physiological reactions and the reactions of the fetus (DiPietro, 2010).

Research indicates that the mother's state may have a more long-term effect. Several studies have found a relationship between stress and anxiety in mothers during pregnancy and the temperament of newborns and their later reactions to new experiences, as well as attentional and behavioral problems (Gutteling et al., 2005, 2006). A large longitudinal study found that mothers' prenatal anxiety and depression predicted elevated internalizing problems through childhood and adolescence (O'Donnell et al., 2014). Another study found that a number of stressful life events during pregnancy predicted both internalizing and externalizing problems, suggesting that the amount of maternal stress matters (Robinson et al., 2011). In addition, studies have found associations between maternal depression and fetal growth and activity, but the correlations are generally small (Field, 2011). Children seem to be particularly vulnerable to maternal stress during the first part of prenatal life; during later stages of pregnancy, maternal stress seems to have less impact on the child's development, but this may be due to the fact that maternal responsiveness to stressful events gradually dampens over time owing to pregnancy-related physiological changes in stress-sensitive hormones (Lazinski et al., 2008; Robinson et al., 2011).

On the other hand, it has been suggested that non-optimal prenatal experiences do not have exclusively negative effects, but can prepare the child and contribute to more flexibility and adaptability in a somewhat "difficult" environment after birth (Pluess & Belsky, 2011). It is also possible that mothers who react more emotionally to different situations provide a more varied and stimulating physiological environment for the fetus (DiPietro, 2010).

Fetal development is complex, and the interpretation of causal relationships in these types of studies is associated with considerable uncertainty. Statistical correlation says nothing about what is cause and what is effect. Development is transactional during fetal life as well (DiPietro, 2010). Depression and anxiety can lead mothers to smoke and drink more alcohol, substances which can affect the development of the fetus (see Chapter 8, this volume). Mothers with fetuses that are active or have developmental anomalies can experience pregnancy as more stressful. Studies showing increased stress in mothers of children with Down syndrome or cleft palate point in this direction (Drillien & Wilkinson, 1964; Stott, 1973). Such conditions cannot possibly have been triggered by the mother's emotional state. Furthermore, mothers who are depressed or stressed during pregnancy tend to maintain these states after birth. It is therefore difficult to separate the effects of stress during pregnancy from the consequences of the mother's stress level and possible interaction problems during the child's first months of life (Field, 2011; Mulder et al., 2002).

It is sometimes argued that experiences during a normal birth can have a profound effect on children's development and lead to mental problems later in life (Winnicott, 1992). There is no scientific support for such claims, and others argue that the powerful forces associated with labor and delivery fulfill an adaptive role that helps the newborn child begin to function independently and thereby eases the transition from fetus to infant (Hepper, 1992; Ronca & Alberts, 1995).

Summary of Part II

1   Development begins at conception. The characteristics and abilities of a child at birth emerge as the result of 9 months of development. The *germinal period* consists of the first 10 days. The 6 weeks following the germinal period are called the *embryonic period*, while the *fetal period* lasts until the child is born.

2   Several diseases can affect fetal development. In addition to the mother's use of alcohol, tobacco and drugs, chemical substances in the environment have also proved to be of importance. The particular effect of various substances depends on when and for how long the fetus has been exposed to them.

3   The sensory systems develop in a fixed order, and all senses are functional by week 26. Gradually, the fetus changes in its reactions to stimulation.

4   After about 7 weeks, the fetus begins to move and performs up to 20,000 movements per day by week 16. Following this, the inactive periods last progressively longer. Activity strengthens the body of the fetus, develops its senses, provides feedback about its physical growth and forms the basis for the behavior the child shows at birth.

5   Sensory stimulation of the fetus helps to activate the nervous system. On the whole, the fetal environment is characterized by repetitive and non-specific types of stimulation in preparation for the more intense and varied stimulation the child will meet after birth.

6   During the fetal period, learning can take place by means of habituation and exposure, but it is uncertain when the human fetus is sufficiently developed to form associations through conditioning. Newborns are more attentive to their mother's voice than the voices of strangers and must therefore have formed some kind of memory of the maternal voice.

7   It is assumed that the course of fetal development has a certain bearing on the child's future development, "fetal programming" and epigenesis. There is a certain continuity in fetal activity, and a correlation between fetal reactions to stimulation and temperament during infancy. This can increase the probability of children attending to their own mother.

8   The mother's emotional state during pregnancy can affect the child's later development. For example, there is a relationship between the mother's emotions and fetal growth and activity, especially during the first part of fetal development, but the correlations are generally small, and it is difficult to distinguish prenatal influences from later ones. On the other hand, fetuses whose mothers react more emotionally to different situations may have a more varied and stimulating physiological environment. Fetal development is complex, and the interpretation of causal relationships in these types of studies is associated with considerable uncertainty.

9   There is no scientific support for the claim that particular experiences during birth can have a profound effect on a child's development and lead to psychiatric disorders later in life.

Core Issues

- The influence of fetal experiences on later development.
- The influence of the mother's mental state on the fetus and the child's later development.

Suggestions for Further Reading

Behnke, M., Smith, V. C., & Committee on Substance Abuse (2013). Prenatal substance abuse: Short- and long-term effects on the exposed fetus. *Pediatrics*, *131*, e1009–e1024.

James, D. K. (2010). Fetal learning: A critical review. *Infant and Child Development*, *19*, 45–54.

O'Connor, T. G., Monk, C., & Fitelson, E. M. (2014). Practitioner review: Maternal mood in pregnancy and child development – implications for child psychology and psychiatry. *Journal of Child Psychology and Psychiatry*, *55*, 99–111.

Part III

Brain Development

11

Brain and Mind

The brain is the central organ responsible for human mental prowess, and its structure and large size relative to body size are defining features of *Homo sapiens* (Neubauer & Hublin, 2012). Ever since the birth of developmental psychology, an important goal has been to understand how the brain performs various functions and why it develops as it does (Preyer, 1882). There are searches for neurological processes that correspond with the various theoretical views on cognitive, social and emotional functions (e.g., Adolphs, 2009; Becker, 2006; Mahy et al., 2014; Meissner, 2008). Cultural differences are to some extent viewed in the context of brain development as well (Chiao et al., 2010). New technologies have led to an increasing use of brain function measurements in studies of both typical and atypical development (see Mareschal et al., 2007a, b; Nelson et al., 2006b). Understanding of brain structure and function and their development – and of the relationship between brain and mind – remains fairly limited, however (Miller, 2010). It is not likely that the human mind and the human brain are organized in the same way (Dekker & Karmiloff-Smith, 2011; Thomas et al., 2013). The basis for mapping the brain's functions is provided by psychological models that tell researchers what to look for.

DOI: 10.4324/9781003292456-14

12

Methods of Studying the Brain

In order to find out how the brain is built up and performs various tasks, researchers investigate the brains of children who develop normally; search for the causes of **attention deficit disorder**, intellectual disability, autism spectrum disorder and other severe developmental disorders; and examine the functional consequences of cerebral hemorrhage and other physical damage in the brain of people who previously functioned normally (Dennis & Thompson, 2013). Many studies have aimed to find out which parts of the brain and neural networks are involved in performing various mental functions. The most important methods are electroencephalography and magnetic resonance imaging, which make it possible to examine the brain while the subject performs various mental tasks (Brown & Jernigan, 2012; Hunt & Thomas, 2008).

Electroencephalography (EEG) is administered by attaching 20 or more sensors to the exterior of the head to record the electrical activity in the cerebral cortex. *Magnetoencephalography* (MEG) uses magnetic sensors inside a helmet to measure brain currents. The electrical activity of nerve cells, or neurons, creates weak magnetic fields, and, when many thousands of neurons are activated simultaneously, it is possible to measure the magnetic field they create on the surface of the skull using MEG. EEG and MEG are often used to measure how the brain responds to sensory stimulation. The brain's response to visual stimulation is registered by measuring the activity in the visual cortex. Response to auditory stimulation is measured by placing sensors over the part of the cortex that processes auditory stimuli (Picton & Taylor, 2007). The *mismatch response* (MMR) is an example of such a use of EEG. MMR is a brain wave that appears 100–150 milliseconds after the subject has been exposed to an unknown or unexpected

DOI: 10.4324/9781003292456-15

sound (Näätänen, 2003). The method can be used to assess whether a child recognizes or expects a particular sound, similar to **dishabituation** after habituation (see Book 1, *Theoretical Perspectives and Methodology*, Chapter 25).

Magnetic resonance imaging (MRI) produces black-and-white images of the shape and size of the brain. Because MRI is sensitive to the cell differences in various types of tissues, such as white and gray brain matter, the images provide information about the structure of the brain and the composition of different tissue types. The brain depends on oxygen supplied by the blood, and blood flow is regulated

Child with EEG sensors

so that active areas receive more oxygen. MRI can detect the oxygen level in the blood – whether it is oxygen-rich or oxygen-depleted – and provides a signal called BOLD (blood-oxygen-level-dependent). **Functional magnetic resonance imaging** (fMRI) measures oxygen content or changes in oxygen content in different areas of the brain while the child (or adult) performs a specific task, such as looking at something, listening to something or doing mental arithmetic. The oxygen level in the blood is measured and compared with the oxygen level when the child is at rest or performs another task. MRI provides information about the brain's structural composition, and fMRI provides information about whether one or more areas are active while the child is processing sensory stimulation or performing a specific task, such as talking or recognizing an object (Hunt & Thomas, 2008).

These methods are technically quite complex. They have different strengths and weaknesses and supplement each other. fMRI provides precise information about active localizations, but results in inaccurate temporal data because the measurements are limited by the inertia of blood circulation and metabolism. Additionally, blood flow can be affected by factors that have nothing to do with the task at hand. EEG and MEG can measure the electrical activity in the brain down to a few milliseconds, but, because measurement is done from the outside and only a small portion of the electrical impulses are registered, it can be difficult to determine where the signal stems from (Hari & Kujala, 2009; Mareschal et al., 2007a).

13

Brain Structure

The brain contains neurons, the specialized cells of the nervous system, each consisting of a *cell body* (nucleus), an axon and a substantial number of dendrites. The **axon** is a long, thin nerve fiber that sends impulses from the neuron to other cells. Although each neuron only has a single axon, it usually has many extensions, and can therefore reach up to several thousand other neurons. **Dendrites** are short, branch-like projections of the neuron whose function is to receive impulses from the axons of surrounding neurons, muscle cells or glands. The number of dendrites determines the number of cells from which a neuron can receive electrical impulses. The adult brain consists of some 86 billion cells and 150 trillion cell connections (Liao et al., 2017).

Nerve impulses are electrochemical signals that travel in the form of an electrical **action potential** at a speed of up to 300 kilometers per hour. The transition point between cells is called a synapse, and the small vesicles at the end of the axon are synaptic terminals. The electrical impulse triggers chemical compounds called **neurotransmitters** that are picked up by *receptors* on the receiving neuron and briefly affect its activity. The effect of neurotransmitters can be *excitatory* (activating), meaning that the receiving nerve reacts more easily. They can also be *inhibitory*, making it more difficult for the nerve to pass on impulses. Inhibitory neurotransmitters are essential for the brain in order to suppress irrelevant information. Excitation and **inhibition** make up the brain's two basic processes, and the sum of all excitatory and inhibitory impulses that reach a neuron determines its activity (Brodal, 2004). The function of neurotransmitters is determined by genes as well as experience (see Chapter 15, this volume).

The central nervous system consists of the spinal cord, the cerebrum and the **cerebellum** (Figure 13.1). The cerebral cortex is about 2–5

DOI: 10.4324/9781003292456-16

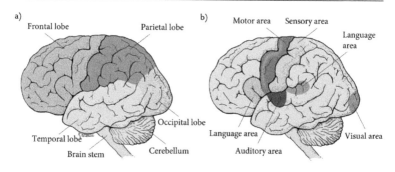

Figure 13.1 The brain.

(a) The cerebrum, the cerebellum and the brain stem. The cerebrum consists of two roughly equal parts connected by a broad band of nerve fibers in the *corpus callosum* and is typically divided into four main areas: the top, front part is occupied by the *frontal lobes*, which are located in front of the *central sulcus*. The remaining parts of the brain lie behind this fold. The *parietal lobes* are located right behind the center of the head, while the *occipital lobes* occupy the lowest part and the back. The *temporal lobes* lie furthest down on the side of the head. (b) Parts of the left brain hemisphere that are particularly important for the development of perception, motor skills and language.

millimeters thick and forms the outer layer of the brain. It consists of some 20 billion cells, each of which on average is connected to more than 1,000 other cells. The different parts of the brain fulfill various tasks and functions that are distributed in all directions: some functions involve the anterior part of the brain in particular, while others take place in the middle or the back, near the surface or further down, in the right or left hemisphere, and so on. Yet, none of these functions take place in one specific location. Just like the body, the brain constitutes a whole whose various parts work together (see the following).

The brain is not a model of the body. There is no direct and precise correspondence between the sensory and motor areas of the cerebral cortex and different parts of the body. Neurons responsible for adjacent body areas are often clustered around the same area. Cells that control the arm, elbow and shoulder for example can all work together, but not with cells that deal with the face and the body. Muscles that are used at the same time are thus controlled by the same area. This is a useful arrangement that facilitates a coordinated activation of neurons leading to the muscles that perform the complex movements of the arm. Although different movements generate different activation patterns, many of the same neural connections are involved (Barinaga, 1995).

14

The Brain and Experience

The brain has a biological basis that evolved through evolution but depends on activity in order to develop (Cicchetti, 2002). Any minor or major new skill, experience or insight that is maintained involves the organization of cellular groups and processes. An individual's experiences affect the thickness, height, length and weight of the brain. Wild animals have larger brains than domesticated animals, probably because they have grown up in an environment with more varied activities. This cannot be caused by genetic differences, because the offspring of wild animals growing up in captivity have smaller brains than those growing up freely in their natural environment (Schrott, 1997). Similarly, the cerebral cortex of children who have suffered neglect and early institutionalization is thinner than that of children who have grown up under normal conditions (Belsky & de Haan, 2011).

Experience affects the brain in various ways. Bourgeois (1997) describes the development of the cerebral cortex as progressing from experience-independent to experience-expectant processes, followed by experience-dependent processes. *Experience-independent* processes are controlled by genes and conditions in the organism and are not dependent on stimulation. They mostly take place during the fetal period.

Experience-expectant processes depend on external stimulation that is present in most human environments and they thus contribute to a similar design of the cerebral cortex in all humans who grow up under normal conditions. *Synaptogenesis* – the formation of new synapses – is predetermined, but the functional efficiency of many networks of neurons requires that they are activated in the right way at the right time. If the environment does not offer the expected experiences – as

DOI: 10.4324/9781003292456-17

for example in cases of parental neglect – the result can be atypical brain development (Belsky & de Haan, 2011; Cicchetti, 2002).

Experience-dependent processes become prominent later in development. They involve the development of networks of cells and synapses as the result of experience and thus represent adaptation to the child's ecology. The more or less unique experiences of children affect the way in which the brain perceives and processes stimulation and initiates action and thus contribute to individual differences in brain development and functioning (Cicchetti, 2002; Lewis, 2005).

15

Brain Development

The development of the brain is a complex process that begins when the fetus is about 2 weeks old and continues all the way into adulthood, involving complementary processes of *producing* as well as *eliminating* neurons and neural connections. Brain development also includes **cell migration**, **myelination** and **specialization** (see below).

Prenatal Development

The brain and the rest of the nervous system evolve from the outer layer of the embryo. After 2–3 weeks, this area begins to form an embryonic disc, which folds together into a closed neural tube. The cells in this tube produce new cells at an average rate of 250,000 *per minute* until birth (Ackerman, 1992). Gradually, the tube divides into layers, and cellular functions become more differentiated.

Cell Migration

The overall structure of the brain is the same for all human beings. It is largely determined by genetic factors and has to do with which parts of the body the different areas of the brain are associated with. An important question is what causes cells to migrate and to specialize (see below). The instructions for cells to move to a particular area at the right time is probably part of the overall genetic blueprint, but this does not depend on the production of special cell types for each area by means of cell division. The cells are guided by other cells as well as chemical substances in the developing brain that cause certain neurons to cluster together and drive out foreign cells. This is how cells build up the brain from the inside out – at first there is nothing special about the cells that will perform a particular function, but, as soon as they

DOI: 10.4324/9781003292456-18

arrive where they are supposed to do their work, they begin to specialize. Experimental studies with animals in which cells were moved early
during development show that cells from the brain's visual area begin
to "hear" when they are moved to the area that is in charge of sound.
Chemical compounds from the surrounding tissues stimulate further
development within the cells. Therefore, the specialization of individual
cells is the result of development rather than a cause of it (Evrard et al.,
1997). Cell migration is at its most active during fetal development, and
most cells have found their place by the time a child is born.

The development of the cerebral cortex begins when the fetus is
8 weeks old and continues until birth. At 6 months, it is completely
smooth, at 7 months it shows traces of folds, and at birth the folds are
almost fully formed (Figure 15.1).

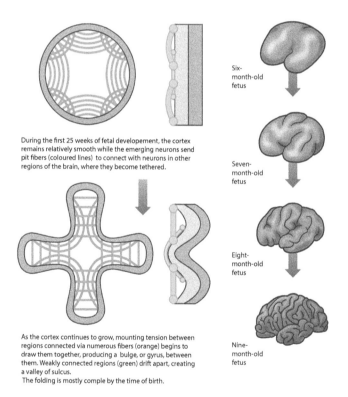

During the first 25 weeks of fetal developement, the cortex
remains relatively smooth while the emerging neurons send
pit fibers (coloured lines) to connect with neurons in other
regions of the brain, where they become tethered.

As the cortex continues to grow, mounting tension between
regions connected via numerous fibers (orange) begins to
draw them together, producing a bulge, or gyrus, between
them. Weakly connected regions (green) drift apart, creating
a valley of sulcus.
The folding is mostly comple by the time of birth.

Six-
month-old
fetus

Seven-
month-old
fetus

Eight-
month-old
fetus

Nine-
month-old
fetus

Figure 15.1 The folds of the cerebral cortex.

The folds of the cerebral cortex are formed during the last 3 months of fetal development (based on Hilgetag & Barbas, 2009, p. 68).

Brain Development in Childhood

The main structure of the brain is present at birth, and the further development is characterized by the creation of smaller and larger functional networks. Figuratively speaking, the brain's "hardware" develops first, while new networks – the brain's "software" – are added and updated throughout childhood and adolescence (Liao et al., 2017; Menon, 2013; see Box 15.1).

Box 15.1   Essential Phases of Brain Development (based on Ackerman, 1992, p. 88; Menon, 2013, p. 628)

1   Proliferation of a vast number of undifferentiated brain cells.
2   Migration of the cells toward a predetermined location in the brain and the beginning of their differentiation into the specific type of cell appropriate to that location.
3   Aggregation of similar types of cells into distinct regions.
4   Formation of innumerable connections among neurons, segregation of functional circuits.
5   Dynamic pruning of functional circuits.
6   Reconfiguration: functional connectivity within and between spatially independent, large-scale functional networks undergoes significant changes with development.
7   Competition among cells and connections results in the stabilization of the 86 billion cells and 150 trillion connections or so that remain.

Size

The brain of a newborn weighs about 20 percent of an adult brain and has 25 percent of its volume. Its weight increases rapidly however, from about 300 grams at birth to 900 grams at the age of 1 year – 60 percent of the weight of an adult brain. At the age of 6, its volume has reached 90 percent, and, at age 10, the weight of the brain is about the same as that of an adult, on average 1,400 grams for men and 1,250 grams for women. But there is significant variation. A survey of 200 people aged 17–40 showed a range from 1,120 to 1,780 grams for men, and 1,070 to 1,550 grams for women (Stiles et al., 2015).

The thickness of the cerebral cortex increases by one-third in the first 2 years, reaching 97 percent of adult thickness. The cortical surface area more than doubles but still constitutes only about 70 percent of the adult surface at 2 years (Lyall et al., 2015).

Myelination

This is the formation of a layer of proteins and fat (myelin) around the nerve fibers. Myelin acts as an insulator, tripling the conduction velocity (up to 120 meters per second) and increasing the cells' efficiency and precision (Ackerman, 1992). Myelination begins during the fourth month of gestation, but has barely gotten started at birth and takes many years to complete. The process starts in the evolutionarily older neural pathways that manage the swallowing reflex and other basic functions. The sensory pathways are often myelinated before those responsible for motor functions. Myelination of the cerebral cortex happens last, beginning right after birth and continuing all the way into early adulthood. Furthermore, many axons remain unmyelinated (Couperus & Nelson, 2006). Since the number of neurons decreases during development (see below), the increase in weight must be caused by the myelination and the continuing growth of the remaining neurons and their dendrites.

Production and Reduction of Cells and Connections

The function of the brain is to keep experiences for later use, and every single experience forms new synaptic patterns. During fetal development and early infancy, the brain overproduces cells, and, in early infancy, the brain has more neurons than at any other time in life. About half of the cells gradually disappear as the result of "**cell death**," a selective elimination of cells based on maturation and experience.

At birth, there are relatively few cell connections or synapses, but their number increases rapidly (Figure 15.2). Areas associated with the basic functions of perception and motor skills develop first, followed by associative skills, while areas central to learning and cognition develop last. The temporal differences in developmental progress help to divide tasks between the various parts of the brain (see below, p. 000). The visual cortex grows rapidly at 3–4 months of age, and in the period 4–12 months the synaptic density is 50 percent higher than in adults (Huttenlocher, 1990; Johnson, 1998). The extent of this process can be illustrated by the fact that the brain of a new-born macaque monkey forms about 40,000 new synapses in the visual cortex *every second* (Bourgeois, 1997). The brain of the human child forms several trillion excess connections. It would not be economical to keep all experiences that have formed a synaptic pattern. The connections between simultaneously activated neurons are strengthened, while inactive synapses disappear, resulting in a significant amount of **synaptic pruning** (Casey et al., 2005). This process generally begins at around 6–7 months of age, but the exact time varies between the different areas of the cerebral cortex (Rakic et al., 1986). In some areas it happens right after birth, in others at 2 years of age. Around 4 years, the number of connections is at its highest.

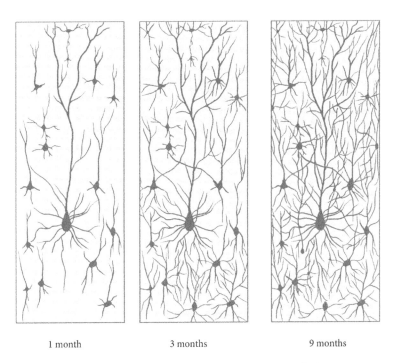

1 month   3 months   9 months

Figure 15.2 Development of neurons and synapses in the cerebral cortex.

New neurons are created, and the number of connections between them increases during the first months of life.

The large number of cells and synapses means that learning conditions are ideal early in life, but the brain would be fairly inefficient if it were to hold on to every single experience or action. The purpose of reducing the number of neurons and synapses is to strengthen those that persist and avoid expending energy on maintaining functions that are of little relevance. Nerve connections compete with each other so that the strong cells (frequently used) survive and the weak ones (rarely used) disappear. The cells that are much used are those that help the organism achieve its goals. The motivational and emotional state of the organism affects the cells' receptivity and is of importance to learning and the particular neural connections that are established. As a number of basic brain functions are less dependent on experience, fewer synapses are pruned away in their locations.

The brain needs energy to produce and reduce cells and synapses, and metabolic processes provide the cells with the energy needed. In the child's first year of life, the brain's metabolism is about 50–70 percent lower than in adults. At age 2, it is the same as in adults but continues to increase and reaches a peak around age 4, shortly after the number of synaptic connections is at its highest. At this age, children have twice as many neural connections as adults, after which the number gradually drops to an adult level. In most areas of the brain, the metabolism reaches adult levels by the age of 9, but in some areas it remains higher throughout adolescence (Johnson, 1998). This shows that the brain uses a great deal of energy to process stimulation and develop its various functions.

The enormous number of cells and synapses demonstrates the sheer workload involved in "producing" the brain of a human being, and the complexity of the neurodevelopmental process. It also demonstrates that experience is a necessary part of the process, not least because the 15,000 genes involved in the functioning of the brain are not enough to define such a complex structure in finite detail (de Haan & Johnson, 2003).

Brain Development in Adolescence

The period from adolescence to early adulthood is regarded as a transitional period constituting a second peak of human brain development (Zhong et al., 2017). There is considerable myelination, especially of the frontal parts, and reorganization of the brain. Many of the connections established in childhood are removed (Konrad et al., 2013). During puberty, pruning reduces synapses by 40 percent. As many as

10,000 synapses can be pruned every second in the prefrontal cortex once the decline in the number of synapses begins to exceed the formation of new synapses in early adolescence (Dawson, 1994; Lewis, 2005). The synaptic density of the prefrontal area reaches a comparable density to that of adults at 10–20 years of age (Huttenlocher, 1990; Johnson, 1998). The fine-tuning of overall connections continues into adulthood (Khundrakpam et al., 2013; Váša et al., 2017). There is a reduction in short-range connections and a strengthening of long-range connections, and functions are less defined to a local network and more to a network independent of location (Grayson & Fair, 2017).

The protracted development of the human prefrontal cortex during adolescence has been proposed to underlie the maturation of cognitive functions and the regulation of affective responses (Caballero et al., 2016), together with the influence from gonadal hormones during puberty, affecting the structuring of the adolescent brain (Guyer et al., 2016). Adolescent brain development is characterized by an imbalance caused by an earlier maturation of systems related to rewards and the not yet fully mature prefrontal control system. This imbalance may be the neural basis for the typical emotional reactive style of adolescence and it may promote risky behavior (Konrad et al., 2013). These changes are assumed to be a basis for adolescents' increased susceptibility to social and emotional experiences and peer influence and play a role in the higher frequency of anxiety and depressive disorders typical of adolescence (Guyer et al., 2016; Mills, 2015).

Specialization

It is a characteristic of the adult brain that there are areas that are particularly important for the performance of certain tasks or functions (see p. 000). The cerebellum, for example, is important for the performance of coordinated movements, as well as cognitive and affective regulation. The visual cortex is essential for interpreting and understanding visual impressions, and the auditory cortex for interpreting and understanding sounds. Some brain systems are involved in many cognitive tasks, such as attention, monitoring and maintaining goals. They also ensure that a number of tasks are executed while special systems are being developed to deal with them (Baillieux et al., 2008; Poldrack, 2010). Progressive specialization contributes to the increase in complexity that characterizes brain development in general (Stiles et al., 2015).

The question is, what causes the brain's organization? From a nativist point of view, the brain contains many innate **modules** whose predetermined functions emerge as a result of maturation (see Book 4, *Cognition, Intelligence and Learning*, Chapter 5). At the other extreme, the brain's organization is seen as the result of learning. Between these two extremes lies the view that the brain's organization is the result of an evolutionary process involving existing connections between different regions of the brain, and between the brain and the body. From this point of view, the brain has a body. It is not an isolated entity, but develops functionally through the body, which in turn both affects and becomes affected by the environment (Marshall, 2016).

There is a widespread and coordinated change in brain connectivity across much of the brain during the first two decades of life (Menon, 2013). Studies show that younger children often activate a larger area of the brain than older children when performing the same task, and many connections appear random (Johnson et al., 2009). In the early years, children develop many "small world networks" with high local clustering and short path length (Liao et al., 2017). Increasingly, the messages between these cell systems allow the brain's functions to be carried out by the areas best suited to the task, consolidating them and ensuring their survival. When adult brains show *less* activation in specialized areas than those of children, it may be owing to the fact that they have developed specialized systems that are smaller and more efficient. Once specialization has taken place, including cell death and synaptic pruning, new cognitive functions are the result not merely of activating smaller areas in the cerebral cortex, but equally of a renewed collaboration between specialized cellular systems and areas. Under such circumstances, the adult brain sometimes activates more systems than that of a child.

The brains of children thus show little specialization to begin with. With a basis in both genetic influences and experience, they develop a number of specialized systems that are organized into integrated networks capable of solving increasingly complex tasks (Tomasi & Volkow, 2011). It is an efficient and **self-organizing** system: the brain is shaped by its own activity (Sirois et al., 2008).

Lateralization

Lateralization means that certain functions are allocated to one of the cerebral hemispheres and is a core element in the brain's specialization. Each hemisphere primarily controls perception and motor skills in the opposite side of the body, but also fulfills functions not directly related to perception or motor skills. Injury to the left hemisphere, for example, often causes language impairments in adults, while injury to the right hemisphere typically affects spatial perception. However, studies have found little relation between lateralization and language skills in children, and weak lateralization may be a consequence rather than a cause of impaired language learning (Bishop, 2013).

A certain degree of functional lateralization is already present during the embryonic period, and the differences become more pronounced with age. The perception of language and faces for example seems to activate areas in both hemispheres during early development, but later mostly on one side alone (Geschwind & Galaburda, 1985; Karmiloff-Smith, 2010).

When only one of the hemispheres assumes a specific function, it may be owing to a difference in the pace of development. As the brain does not have the capacity to develop all areas simultaneously, it constantly prioritizes some areas in favor of others. Areas that are ready to perform a given task in one hemisphere attend to this task. Lateralization thus does not originate in a functional genetic specification of different areas of the brain, but is the result of temporal regulation and prioritizing certain areas and processes (Johnson, 2011). This allows for flexibility during development and may explain why lateralization is reversed or uncertain in some people. Nearly all right-handers have important centers for processing language in their left hemisphere, while a third of all left-handers have similar centers on the right side (Bishop, 2013). For example, other parts of the brain can take over in case those normally used have been damaged (see below). This kind of functional transfer would not be possible if functions were hardwired to a specific area. The temporal organization of different processes, however, depends on genetic information. Thus, the development of the brain itself is largely predetermined, but the developmental process is subject to environmental factors and any possible injury. This makes it possible for children to grow up and cope under very different conditions.

Mirror Neurons

The brain is a receiving as well as an executive organ. It processes and interprets sensory impressions, and plans and regulates actions. **Mirror neurons** are activated both when an action is carried out and when the same action is observed (seen, heard or felt) (Gallese et al., 1996;

Hunter et al., 2013). However, the term "mirror" is not a particularly fitting analogy. It is not enough to observe a movement: mirror neurons are only activated once the *intention* of a physical action becomes apparent. The cells are not activated by a "vacant" stretching motion alone, for example, but only once the goal of the movement becomes evident, such as taking a glass of water. Nor is it only the sight of the movement that can activate the cells, as the term "mirror neurons" seems to suggest: in addition, the sounds usually associated with an action lead to an activation of the cells. Therefore, mirror neurons do not function as a mirror reflection of an action but rather as a concept-forming mechanism that includes various aspects of a given action (Jacob, 2009, 2013).

There has been much discussion about the significance of mirror neurons for human development. Some claim that this type of mirroring is necessary in order to understand or imitate the actions of others and experience **empathy**. It allows humans to understand the actions of others "from the inside" – as if they were their own (Rizzolatti & Sinigaglia, 2010). Others are sceptical of such an interpretation and point out that mirror neurons are not unique to human beings. Therefore, the presence of these cells does not explain the development of exclusively human functions (Hickok, 2013; Steinhorst & Funke, 2014).

There is also disagreement about the development of mirror neuron systems. Some believe they are genetically determined, and that observing and executing an action will automatically lead to the activation of the same cells (Fogassi & Ferrari, 2011). An alternative explanation is that mirror neuron systems originate through learning via the concerted execution and observation of an action (Cook et al., 2014). At present, the results of studies of mirror neurons do not distinguish between different explanations of cognitive development (Caramazza et al., 2014).

Mirror neurons represent an important discovery, showing that the brain has complex and efficient mechanisms to identify important environmental conditions and facilitate action. At the same time, it illustrates the difficulties of transferring knowledge about the brain in order to draw conclusions about the mind.

The Brain Functions as a Whole

Although some brain areas are specialized to a certain degree, the brain nevertheless functions as a whole. The cerebral cortex changes with context, experience and expectation, and rarely is a task done in one location alone – several areas are usually necessary for a function to be performed (Singer, 2013). Even a simple event such as the unexpected sound of a flute leads to the activation of 24 different brain areas (Kagan, 2007).

Activation of the frontal lobes is affected by many other parts of the brain and illustrates that the division of labor is a complex process. Emotional regulation includes intention, planning, **communication**, motor skills and behavior, and one of the tasks of the frontal lobes is to coordinate these processes. The right frontal lobe is more associated with negative affects such as agitation, anxiety, crying and withdrawal, and the left with joy, interest, anger and approach behavior. However, they are not symmetrical: a high level of activation in one of the frontal lobes does not lead to a low level of activation in the other. They represent different emotional qualities, and it is the combined pattern of activation between the two areas that determines an individual's emotional reactions (Johnson et al., 2009; Nelson & Bosquet, 2000).

The brain's division of labor requires cooperation. Areas that need to collaborate on sensory input, actions involving both sides of the body or different functional tasks must be able to communicate efficiently. A substantial increase in connections between the two brain hemispheres takes place from 3 to 6 years of age. Reduced capacity of these connections can lead to delayed development and also seems to be associated with a number of developmental disorders (Horwitz & Horovitz, 2012).

16

Early and Later Plasticity

Plasticity refers to the brain's ability to change as a result of experience. Many areas of the brain are more *plastic* or more *malleable* during early development than later in life (Kolb et al., 2013). The functions of many areas of the brain are not yet finally determined, and the course of development can follow somewhat different paths (Menon, 2013). This opens up other alternatives in case a particular **developmental path** is closed owing to defect or injury. Both children and adults can experience illness or accidents that result in injury to the brain, but children often have a better prognosis than adults. In some areas, injuries in children barely seem to have any developmental consequences. In fact, it is possible to remove one brain hemisphere at an early age without severe consequences for language and cognitive functions, and in special cases it can lead to better functioning when the hemisphere is removed because the child has epilepsy that cannot be controlled with medication (Battro, 2000; Bulteau et al., 2017; Immordino-Yang, 2007; Vargha-Khadem et al., 1997; see Box 16.1).

It is assumed that damaged areas in the brains of children heal more easily (restitution), and that "vacant" areas are able to assume the tasks of areas that have been injured (substitution). However, there is considerable variation in the development of children following brain injury (Anderson et al., 2011). Children with brain damage often show difficulties and disorders in many areas. When the removal of a hemisphere leads to more typical development, the reason may be that the child's functions have mainly developed in the good hemisphere, and removal of the bad hemisphere takes away the pathological processes related to the epilepsy.

DOI: 10.4324/9781003292456-19

Box 16.1   A Child with Half a Brain
(Borgstein & Grootendorst, 2002)

A girl had a hemispherectomy (removal of one hemisphere) at the age of 3 for Rasmussen syndrome because intractable epilepsy had led to right-sided hemiplegia and severe **regression** of language skills (see photograph). Though the dominant hemisphere was removed, with its centers for language and motor control of the left side of her body, at 7 years her hemiplegia has partially recovered and is only noticeable by a slight spasticity of her left arm and leg. She had normal hearing in both ears but a reduced field of vision which she was not aware of (Haak et al., 2014). She was fully bilingual in Turkish and Dutch, attended school and was leading a normal life. She scored low on intelligence tests (IQ 50) but gave an impression of higher potential once she was moved from a special school to mainstream school, and her general school performance improved remarkably.

Thanks to Johannes Borgstein for photograph and supplementary information.

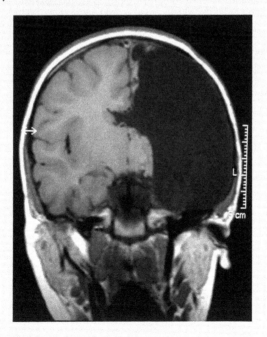

Later difficulties do not always involve functions normally located in the injured area. One study found that children who had experienced brain injury showed improvement over a long time, but that the development of some children seemed to come to a halt when they reached the level at which the injury had occurred. They regained much of what they had learned before the injury, but had great difficulties coping with tasks above the level of the corresponding school grade (Basser, 1962). A possible explanation may be that an area assuming the functions of a damaged area usually fulfills a different function and now is unable to follow a normal development because the area usually allocated to that function is completely or partially occupied (Taylor & Alden, 1997). This means that the consequences of an injury may first show up at the age when the new function was to be established. As reorganization may take place at the expense of the later development of a different function, it may be necessary to monitor children's development over a long time in order to assess the possible consequences of an injury.

In the longer term, the consequences of an injury can therefore be more serious for younger children than for older children and adults, as it interferes with a long developmental process. It seems that young children are both more vulnerable *and* sufficiently plastic for many functions to be re-established. Plasticity thus changes in different ways. Some functions are more vulnerable to early injury; others have more serious consequences when they occur later on. The brain is unable to compensate for all functions that may be impaired. Especially basic functions such as motor skills are difficult to compensate for because the areas responsible for these functions are myelinated during early development. Damage to areas having to do with plasticity may lead to a global deterioration that is difficult to counteract. The developmental arrest of girls with Rett syndrome (see Chapter 3, this volume) is an example of such an injury. Moreover, compensation often has a cost, as when the function usually carried out by an area that has taken over the function of a damaged area is not as well developed (Kolb et al., 2013; Pennington, 2015).

Critical and Sensitive Periods

During development there are periods of plasticity when the child has a unique or particularly good opportunity for learning or development.

The organism may require specific forms of stimulation within a certain *time window* to develop the ability to process this stimulation. For example, the development of stereoscopic depth perception depends on the simultaneous stimulation of both eyes during the first years of life (see Book 3, *Perceptual and Motor Development*, Chapter 3). In order to speak a language without an accent, it must be acquired during a time window for phonological categorization (Hensch, 2004; see also Book 5, *Communication and Language Development*, Chapter 6). Following a **critical period**, stimulation is unable to restore functions that were not developed at the right time. However, the plasticity of a critical period may also imply vulnerability to harmful influences. Various periods during fetal development for example are characterized by vulnerabilities to different teratogens (see Chapter 9, this volume).

A **sensitive period** implies a heightened susceptibility to environmental influences: the brain is particularly vulnerable or capable of learning something more easily than during other developmental periods (Roth & Sweatt, 2011). There is a sensitive period for learning language for example. New languages can be learned throughout life, but it seems to be particularly easy from the age of 1 until **school age**. While critical periods are rare, many assumptions have been made about sensitive periods, such as the development of **perception**, **attachment** and personality (Bailey et al., 2001).

One of the key questions is what leads a critical or sensitive period to start and end. From a functional point of view, the brain is unable to keep all opportunities for development open at all times, as this would require too many resources. Instead, the brain creates neural networks for a given area during a specific period. This is not determined by age, and its onset is flexible, with some variation in age. It is the brain's development of other neurological structures and the balance between excitatory and inhibitory neurons that determine when an area is ready for a critical or sensitive period to take place (Takesian & Hensch, 2013).

The purpose of terminating the plasticity of a critical or sensitive period is to save resources and stabilize the functional neurological structures that have been established so they are not easily lost. If the brain has not received a particular stimulation by the time it is ready, development will proceed on the assumption that this stimulation is not significant. The lack of stimulation tells the brain that no systems or resources are necessary to process this type of stimulation. Its resources can be used for something else. Part of the auditory cortex, for example, could be used for visual processing in case a child is deaf (see Chapter 13, this volume). In blind children, the visual cortex is sometimes used for language processing (Pennington, 2015). The same principle that applies to cell death and synaptic pruning also applies to sensitive and critical periods: the neurological structures that are used at the right time will be maintained.

A critical or sensitive period implies that, once the functional organization of the brain has taken place, it may be impossible to reverse the process and assign other functions to established systems. For instance, the brain creates neurological connections for the language or languages a child has been exposed to during the sensitive period of language development and does not maintain the possibility of learning additional languages with similar ease. The brain no longer creates separate neurological structures for new languages; the learning process must make use of previously established language structures. This makes it more difficult to learn other languages later in life, but, as far as the brain is concerned, it is an economical use of resources. Once the critical and sensitive periods have passed, the individual is also more vulnerable to physical injury, as it is more difficult to establish a new function – or replace a lost function – than during periods with more brain plasticity (Takesian & Hensch, 2013).

The regulation of critical and sensitive periods is an extremely complex process that can be affected by many factors. However, these periods are important to children's ability to adapt based on their own prerequisites and the ecological niche they grow up in (Thomas & Johnson, 2008). By keeping or discarding various neurological connections, the brain prepares to cope in the world as it appears to the individual based on his or her experiences. Critical and sensitive periods are a natural consequence of the brain's ability to specialize and adapt, and thus of the development process itself. They also reflect the fact that development is about timing and providing children with the experiences they need to develop at the time they are ready to cope with them (Elman et al., 1996).

Side by side with the establishment of brain structures as the result of interaction between biology and experience, biological processes become more flexible in themselves and thus capable of processing the entire range of individual experiences. To a certain degree, there is an inverse relationship between neurological plasticity and the flexible processing of experiences. Although reduced plasticity makes the brain more vulnerable to physical injury, the developmental outcome takes advantage of a multitude of integrated mechanisms and complex processes that allow the brain to use the sum of all previous experience and knowledge in order to face new challenges in a flexible way.

17

Gender Differences

Gender is an important developmental factor, and studies have investigated whether there are developmental differences in the brain structure and organization of men and women. Female brains reach their maximum volume 3 years earlier than those of males (11 years 6 months and 14 years 6 months) and are on average 9 percent smaller than the brains of men (Lenroot & Giedd, 2006). Studies have also found a somewhat different organization in male and female brains, but the results are uncertain and sometimes contradictory (Fine, 2014). In some areas, women show a lesser degree of lateralization and seem to have somewhat more connections between the brain hemispheres, while men have more connections within each hemisphere itself (Ingalhalikar et al., 2014). This may indicate that women do more processing involving both hemispheres than men do (Kimura, 1992, 1999).

Sex hormones affect the brain's prenatal development, and a small group of girls have a congenital disorder that results in an excess of male hormones during the fetal period. Even with hormone treatment, these girls have a tendency to act more like boys in their selection of toys, such as preferring cars to dolls (see Book 7, *Social Relations, Self-awareness and Identity*, Part IV). They generally score higher than other girls on tasks involving spatial **concepts**, something boys are somewhat better at than girls as well. Studies have found that male sex hormones inhibit the growth of the left hemisphere and give priority to the right hemisphere, a fact that may explain differences in the degree of lateralization and why girls on average are better at language and perform lower at spatial skills than boys (Servin et al., 2003; Swaab, 2007).

DOI: 10.4324/9781003292456-20

Although the brain is affected by sex hormones, there is no such thing as a male or a female brain or one particular gender-specific dimension. Sex hormones affect different areas of the brain in different ways, and each area can be "male" or "female." Every individual brain is a mosaic of neurological structures – some are male, others female, and some are unisex (McCarthy et al., 2015). Besides, many other factors affect the development of males and females. Studies are rarely able to show behavioral differences that correlate with the gender-specific differences in brain connections. It has also been shown that men and women activate somewhat different brain areas when solving identical tasks that both are able to perform equally well.

It is likely that some of the differences between male and female brains are the consequence of developmental factors that appear too early to be the result of social and cultural conditions. At the same time, it is important to emphasize that they represent average values, with a wide range and significant overlap between cognitive and social attributes in boys and in girls. In addition, gender-related factors represent a small proportion of all the biological factors that, along with social and cultural influences, seem to make up the unique set of abilities and interests of each individual boy or girl.

18

Brain Organization and Atypical Development

The development of the human brain is complex and takes many years. The fact that development mostly works out well demonstrates the brain's extraordinary ability to safeguard and adjust. Sometimes, however, the dynamics of brain development can take a wrong turn and lead to "developmental miswiring" – abnormal development of neural connections (Di Martino et al., 2014). The basic processes of brain development are the same in typical and atypical development, and **neuroimaging** studies show that children with cognitive and behavioral disorders have atypical organization and activity in various brain regions (Dennis & Thompson, 2013; Menon, 2013).

It has been suggested that defects in cell proliferation, reduced or abnormal patterns of neural connections, and variation in timing during cell migration, synaptic pruning or the organization of neurological networks may be linked to the development of epilepsy, autism spectrum disorder, conduct disorder and other severe disorders, as well as to the differences in trajectories of these disorders (Jiang et al., 2015; Kolb et al., 2013; Pennington, 2015). Compared with children with typical development, children with Williams syndrome (see Chapter 3, this volume) have 20 percent smaller brain volume and cortical malformations and show atypical chemistry and activity patterns (Karmiloff-Smith, 1998). Girls with Rett syndrome (see Chapter 3, this volume) have many cells and few synapses in the central part of their brain (Bauman et al., 1995), indicating that neither the elimination of cells nor the formation of synapses functions properly. The connections between amygdala (a structure located in the temporal lobes) and the prefrontal cortex are typically immature in children. The finding that maturation of these connections was accelerated in previously institutionalized and maternally deprived children and

DOI: 10.4324/9781003292456-21

adolescents and associated with reduced anxiety reactions was interpreted as an **adaptation** to the early adversity (Gee et al., 2013). Also, other studies have found that neurological networks involving the amygdala may lead to a vulnerability to mood disorders (Pessoa & Adolphs, 2010). Another example is the smaller than normal head circumference of many children who have spent their early childhood in poor institutions. This may be due to a lack of experience-expectant processes required by the brain or an excess of stress hormones with a damaging influence on brain development (Pennington, 2015).

> The vast majority of mental illnesses are conceptualized as neurodevelopmental disorders, rooted in disturbances of typical brain development.
>
> (Di Martino et al., 2014, p. 1335)

Still, particular brain characteristics do not provide a sufficient basis for diagnosis. One cannot simply "translate" cognitive processes into neurological processes, or vice versa. Undoubtedly, many disorders have an atypical neurological basis, and many different factors can influence such a development. Children with neurodevelopmental disorders (see Book 1, *Theoretical Perspectives and Methodology*, Chapter 32) often show signs of several such disorders, and presumably they include some of the same pathological brain processes. Most disorders have yet to be charted when it comes to identifying the point at which atypical connections and activation patterns originate and how they contribute to the development of children's experiences and behavior (Horwitz & Horovitz, 2012; Miller, 2010). Moreover, many different forms of atypical brain connectivity have been associated with, for example, autism spectrum disorders (Kana et al., 2014; Thomas et al., 2016). A developmental disorder is not simply the result of an injury or a defect, but appears gradually as the result of irregular and abnormal processes in brain development (Johnson et al., 2002; Karmiloff-Smith, 2009). Many disorders are neurodevelopmental in the literal sense of the term.

The current presentation is in line with the *neuroconstructivist* approach, which integrates elements from cognitive **constructivism** (see Book 4, *Cognition, Intelligence and Learning*, Chapter 6), neuroscience and computer simulation of developmental processes

(Karmiloff-Smith, 1998; Mareschal et al., 2007a, b). This approach is critical to nativist assumptions about genetically predetermined modules and views the development of the brain (and mind) as a dynamic structure that gradually grows more complex. Although children do not start as a blank slate, basic congenital factors do not determine the brain's final functions, but instead initiate a process that allows the brain to develop based on genetic predisposition and the child's perception and actions. The interaction of genes and experience in brain development can result in typical as well as atypical functioning (Sirois et al., 2008).

19

Stimulating Development

The brain's ability to regulate development and the fact that experience is of significance to its development are important arguments for adopting suitable measures for children with developmental disabilities. Interventions are likely to be effective, and research also suggests that it is important to start at an early age when possible (Grossman et al., 2003).

More difficult, however, is determining what types of experiences are important to children when genetic and other factors increase the probability of atypical brain development. Moreover, intervention may differ with the presence of a sensitive or critical period. When brain plasticity is high, the aim is to promote problem solving that may stimulate the creation of new smaller and larger patterns of neural connections. After the critical period, the aim may be to guide the child to address challenges with means allowed by the established neural connection patterns (Immordino-Yang, 2007; Nahum et al., 2013). Some children need more or less of certain types of stimulation; others need a general increase or reduction in stimulation. Timing is also important, so that stimulation occurs at the right moment during development. Early stimulation is mostly indirect, influencing how people in the environment perceive and react to a child. Thus, the design of early interventions for children at risk of abnormal and delayed neurological development should be based on a **transactional model** (see Book 1, *Theoretical Perspectives and Methodology*, Chapter 6) (Cicchetti, 2002; Sameroff, 2010).

There are a number of commercially available computerized training programs claiming to train the brain and improve general cognitive function, but these claims are controversial, and, although the performance on training tasks may improve, a transfer to everyday functioning mostly lacks empirical support (Owen et al., 2010; Rabipour & Raz, 2012).

DOI: 10.4324/9781003292456-22

Summary of Part III

1   An important task is to identify how the brain works, and psychological models provide the basis for mapping the brain's functions. However, there is no simple relationship between the structure of the brain and the mind.

2   The brain is examined using advanced *electroencephalography* (EEG and MEG) and *magnetic resonance imaging* (MRI and fMRI). MRI and fMRI provide precise localization but inaccurate temporal data, while MEG and EEG result in inaccurate localization and precise time resolution.

3   A neuron consists of a *cell body* (nucleus), an *axon* and a substantial number of *dendrites*. The transition point between cells is called a *synapse*. *Excitation* and *inhibition* are fundamental brain processes, and the activity of a neuron is determined by the excitatory and inhibitory impulses it receives. *The central nervous system* consists of the *brain stem*, the *cerebrum* and the *cerebellum*. The *cerebral cortex* is 2–5 millimeters thick and forms the outer layer of the brain.

4   Experience affects the thickness, height, length and weight of the brain. An environment offering little stimulation results in a smaller brain size than normal upbringing conditions. *Experience-independent* processes are not dependent on stimulation and mostly occur during the fetal period. *Experience-expectant* processes depend on external stimulation for the brain to develop in a typical way. *Experience-dependent* processes are the result of an individual's experiences, represent adaptation to the child's ecology and contribute to individual differences in brain development and functioning.

5   The nervous system evolves from the outer layer of the embryo, forming a neural tube after 2–3 weeks. Cells migrate to different areas at different times, while their functions become more differentiated. The cerebral cortex begins to develop at around 8 weeks,

and the folds are almost fully formed at birth. The weight of the brain at birth is about 20 percent of that of an adult, with 25 percent of its volume. At 6 years of age, its volume has reached 90 percent of that of an adult brain. At 10 years, the brain's weight is the same as in adults. Myelination begins during the fourth month of gestation, but has barely gotten started at birth and takes many years to complete.

6 During fetal development and early infancy, the brain *overproduces* cells. About half of the cells disappear as a result of experience and maturity, with an uneven distribution throughout the brain. Newborns have relatively few *synapses*, but, between the ages of 9 and 24 months, the cerebral cortex has about 50 percent more synaptic connections than that of an adult. Inactive synapses disappear, while the connection between simultaneously activated neurons is strengthened. The reduction in neurons and synapses strengthens those that are left and prevents the brain from using energy on maintaining unused functions.

7 The period from adolescence to early adulthood is a transitional period with considerable myelination and reorganization. The fine-tuning of overall connections continues into adulthood, with a reduction in short-range connections and a strengthening of long-range connections. Adolescent brain development is characterized by an imbalance caused by an earlier maturation of systems related to rewards and the not yet fully mature prefrontal control system, which may play a role in the higher frequency of mood disorders typical of adolescence.

8 The brain functions as a whole, but also distributes its tasks. The two hemispheres control perception and motor skills in the opposite side of the body, and some functions are *lateralized*. A child's brain shows little specialization to begin with but develops a number of specialized systems that are organized into networks capable of solving increasingly complex tasks.

9 "Mirror neurons" are activated both when performing an action and observing an action with the same intention. Some researchers argue that mirror neurons are necessary in order to understand or imitate the actions of others and experience empathy. Others have pointed out that mirror neurons are not unique to human beings and therefore do not explain exclusively human development. There is also disagreement as to whether mirror neurons are genetically determined or originate through experience.

10 Many areas of the brain are more plastic during early development than later in life. Children have a better prognosis than adults when the brain is injured. This may be owing to superior restitution of injured areas or functional substitution by "vacant" areas. However, compensation may lead to slower development or the impairment of other functions. In the longer term, the consequences of some injuries may be more severe for younger children than for older children and adults as they interfere with a long developmental process.

11 A *critical period* entails that the organism needs specific forms of stimulation within a certain *time window* to develop the ability to process it. A *sensitive period* means that the brain is particularly malleable for a certain period of time, and that some things are more easily learned than during other developmental periods. Critical periods are rare; sensitive periods are more common. Critical and sensitive periods save resources and stabilize established functions. They are a natural consequence of the brain's increasing tendency to specialize and adjust.

12 There are some differences in the brain development of men and women. Studies indicate that their brains are somewhat differently organized, but the results are uncertain and sometimes contradictory. The number of connections within and between the hemispheres differs to a certain extent. Some of the differences appear to be related to sex hormones and appear too early to be the result of social and cultural conditions. However, there is no such thing as a male or a female brain: the brain is a mosaic of different "male" and "female" functions, and every individual has a unique mosaic of "masculine" and "feminine" features. There is a wide range of abilities and significant overlap between cognitive and social attributes in boys and in girls.

13 The brain is a complex organ, and many different factors can lead development in the wrong direction. The cause of developmental disorders is as complex as any other development, and developmental disorders emerge gradually as the result of irregular and abnormal processes in the development of the brain. According to neuroconstructivism, basic congenital factors do not determine the brain's final functions, but instead may initiate a process that allows the brain to develop typically or atypically, based on genetic predisposition and the child's perception and action.

14 The brain's ability to regulate development and the fact that experience is of significance to its development are important arguments for adopting suitable measures for children with developmental disabilities. Early stimulation is usually indirect, influencing how people in the environment perceive and react to the child.

Core Issues

- The role of genes and experience in the formation of the brain.
- The development and function of mirror neurons in human **imitation** and action understanding.
- **Gender differences** in brain development.

Suggestions for Further Reading

Ingalhalikar, M., Smith, A., Parker, D., Satterthwaite, T. D., Elliott, M. A., Ruparel, K., Hakonarson, H., Gur, R. E., Gur, R. C., & Verma, R. (2014). Sex differences in the structural connectome of the human brain. *Proceedings of the National Academy of Sciences, 111*, 823–828.

Johnson, M. H., Grossmann, T., & Cohen Kadosh, K. (2009). Mapping functional brain development: Building a social brain through interactive specialization. *Developmental Psychology, 45*, 151–159.

Karmiloff-Smith, A. (1998). Development itself is the key to understanding developmental disorders. *Trends in Cognitive Sciences, 2*, 389–398.

Liao, X., Vasilakos, A. V., & He, Y. (2017). Small-world human brain networks: Perspectives and challenges. *Neuroscience and Biobehavioral Reviews, 87*, 286–300.

Menon, V. (2013). Developmental pathways to functional brain networks: Emerging principles. *Trends in Cognitive Sciences, 17*, 627–640.

Glossary

See subject index to find the terms in the text

Action potential   The repeated discharges that occur when electrochemical impulses are transmitted through the neuron.

Adaptation   Changes that increase the ability of a species or an individual to survive and cope with the environment.

Adolescence   The period between *childhood* and adulthood, age 12–18.

Aggression   Behavior intended to harm living beings, objects or materials.

Allele   One of several variants of the same gene at the same location on a *chromosome*, and controlling the same genetic characteristics.

Angelman syndrome   Genetic syndrome characterized by hyperactivity and severe learning disabilities; caused by a missing part of chromosome pair 15, inherited from the mother; the counterpart to *Prader-Willi syndrome.*

Antisocial behavior   Behavior that shows little concern for other people's feelings and needs, and violates the common social and ethical norms of a culture.

Association   A link, such as between a stimulus and a reaction or action, or between ideas or thoughts.

Attachment   A *behavioral system* that includes various forms of *attachment behavior;* the system is activated when a child finds herself at a shorter or a longer distance from the person she is attached to, and experiences emotions such as pain, fear, stress, uncertainty or anxiety; the term is also used to describe emotional attachment to a caregiver; Attachment can be secure, insecure and disorganized.

Attention deficit disorder; ADD   Characterized by impulsivity, low ability to concentrate on a task, and little sustained attention, may experience problems with emotional regulation, motor coordination, working memory, spatial perception and executive function.

Atypical development   Course of development that differs significantly from the development of the majority of a *population*; see *individual differences* and *typical development*.

Autism spectrum disorder   Neurodevelopmental disorder that appears in the first years of life; characterized by persistent deficits in social skills, communication and language, and by repetitive behavior and restricted interests.

Autosomal chromosome   Chromosome that is not a *sex chromosome*.

Axon   Long, thin neural conductor that transmits impulses to other cells.

Batten disease; Juvenile neuronal ceroid lipofuscinosis (JNCL)   Genetic *autosomal* recessive disease; neurodegenerative disorder with blindness at age 5–15 and development of childhood dementia with decline in cognitive and motor functions.

Behavioral disorder   All forms of behavior that are socially unacceptable in one way or another, such as running away from home, screaming, cursing, messy eating manners, bed-wetting, ritual behavior, excessive dependency, poor *emotion regulation*, *aggression*, fighting and *bullying*.

Behavioral genetics   The study of how genes and the environment affect the development of characteristics such as *intelligence*, *temperament* and *personality*.

Behavioral phenotype   Characteristic pattern of motor, cognitive, language and social characteristics that seem to be related to a known genetic syndrome or the presence of one or more genes.

Behaviorism; Behavior analysis   Group of psychological theories that emphasize the influence of the environment to explain developmental changes.

Cell death   Selective loss of cells during the first years of life due to *maturation* and experience.

Cell migration   The movement of cells to another location that occurs during fetal development.

Cerebellum   Part of the brain located behind and below the occipital lobe of the cerebrum, lying at an angle between the latter and the continuation of the spinal cord in the skull (medulla oblongata).

Childhood   Age 1–12 years.

Chromosomal abnormality   Change in the number or structure of chromosomes.

Chromosome   Thread-shaped formation in the cellular nucleus that carries genes; always occurs in pairs, with 23 pairs in human beings.

Classical conditioning   See *conditioning*.

Cognition   Thinking or understanding; includes some type of perception of the world, storage in the form of mental *representation*, different ways of managing or processing new and stored experiences, and action strategies.

Collectivist culture   Emphasize social values and the individual's responsibility and place in society; see *individualistic culture*.

Communication   Intentional conveyance of thoughts, stories, desires, ideas, emotions, etc., to one or more persons.

Concept   Mental *representation* of a category of objects, events, persons, ideas, etc.

Conditioning   The learning of a specific reaction in response to specific stimuli; includes classical and operant conditioning. In *classical conditioning*, a neutral stimulus is associated with an unlearned or *unconditioned stimulus* that elicits an unlearned or *unconditioned response*, eventually transforming the neutral stimulus into a conditioned stimulus that elicits a conditioned response similar to the unconditioned response. In *operant conditioning*, an action is followed by an event that increases or reduces the probability that the action will be repeated under similar circumstances.

Constraint (in development)   The organism's resistance to change and adaptation to new experiences; often used in connection with the nervous system; see *plasticity*.

Constructivism   Psychological theories based on the notion that an individual constructs his or her understanding of the outside world.

Continuity (in development)   Development in which later ways of functioning build directly on previous functions and can be predicted based on them.

Correlation   Measure of the degree of covariation between two variables, ranging from −1.00 to +1.00; values close to 0.00 show a low degree of correlation; a positive correlation (+) means that a high score on one variable is associated with high score on the other; a negative cor relation (−) indicates that a high score on one variable is associated with a low score on the other.

Cortex   The outermost, folded layer of the brain; *phylogenetically* the most recent part of the human brain.

Critical period   Limited time period in which an individual is especially susceptible to specific forms of positive or negative stimulation and experience; if the stimulation or experience fails to take place during this period, a similar stimulation or experience later in life will neither benefit nor harm the individual to any appreciable extent; see *sensitive period*.

Culture   The particular activities, tools, attitudes, beliefs, values, norms, etc., that characterize a group or a community.

Dendrite   Short, branch-like extension of the cell body that receives impulses from surrounding nerve cells, muscle cells or glands under certain conditions.

Deoxyribonucleic acid (DNA)   The basic building block of genes, comprised of long spiral-shaped and sequential threads of *introns* and *exons*. DNA provides the blueprint for *ribonucleic acid* (RNA), which performs a number of cellular functions, controls the production of new proteins and triggers chemical reactions in the body.

Development   Changes over time in the structure and functioning of human beings and animals as a result of interaction between biological and environmental factors.

Developmental disorder   Disorder that is congenital or appears in *infancy* or *childhood* without the presence of external injuries or similar.

Developmental path   One of several possible courses of development within the same area or domain.

Developmental phase   Time period central to a particular developmental process.

Disability   The difference between an individual's abilities and the demands of the environment.

Dishabituation   Increased response to a new stimulus or aspect of a stimulus following a reduction in response intensity due to repeated presentation of a stimulus; see *habituation*.

Dizygotic twins; Fraternal twins   Twins resulting from two separate fertilized eggs and sharing 50 percent of each other's genes; see *monozygotic twins* (*identical twins*).

Domain   A delimited sphere of knowledge; an area in which something is active or manifests itself.

Dominant gene   Gene that is expressed even though it is inherited from the mother or the father alone, and resulting in a characteristic that will always be expressed; see *genomic imprinting* and *recessive gene.*

Down syndrome; Trisomy 21   Syndrome that causes varying degrees of *intellectual disability*; caused by an error in cell division that results in a partial or complete extra copy of chromosome 21.

Dyslexia   Severe reading and writing disorder, despite adequate sensory and intellectual abilities and appropriate training; see *learning disorder.*

Dyspraxia   Partial or complete inability to perform voluntary movements.

Electroencephalography (EEG)   Method to record the electrical activity of the brain by means of electrodes attached to the exterior of the skull.

Embryonic period   Weeks 2–8 of prenatal development; see *germinal period* and *fetal period.*

Empathy   Feel with someone; emotional reaction similar to the emotion another person is perceived to experience.

Epigenesis   Developmental process by which an individual's genetic dispositions are modified by environmental influences and change the structure and behavior of the organism.

Experiment   Method to test a hypothesis on specific causal relationships or connections. One or several conditions are systematically altered, and the effect is recorded. As many conditions as possible are kept constant in order not to affect the outcome, increasing the probability that the results are solely related to the conditions being studied.

Expressive language   The language that the child produces.

Extroversion   One of the *Big Five personality traits*; the opposite of *introversion.*

Fetal alcohol syndrome (FAS)   Abnormal development caused by the mother's consumption of alcohol or other drugs during pregnancy; common characteristics include a small head, distinctive facial features, malformations of the heart and limbs, *irritability*, attention deficit disorder and *hyperactivity.*

Fetal period   Ninth week of pregnancy until birth; see *embryonic period* and *germinal period.*

Functional magnetic resonance imaging (fMRI)   Method to examine the brain by measuring the oxygen content or changes in oxygen content in different brain areas while the subject performs a specific task, such as looking at something, listening to something or performing mental calculations.

Gender difference; Sex difference   Characteristic, ability or behavior pattern that differs between the two sexes.

Genome   The sum of all genes of an individual.

Genomic imprinting   Activation of a gene depending on whether the gene is inherited from the father or the mother; see *dominant gene* and *recessive gene*.

Genotype   The genetic makeup of an individual; see *phenotype*.

Germinal period   The first 10 days of prenatal development; see *embryonic period* and *fetal period*.

Habilitation   The effort to improve and support functionality, interaction and quality of life for people with congenital or early-acquired disabilities; see *rehabilitation*.

Habituation   Gradual reduction in the intensity of a reaction or response following repeated stimulation; allows an individual to ignore familiar objects and direct attention at new ones.

Heritability estimate   Calculation of heritability based on the difference between the correlations of fraternal and identical twins.

Huntington disease   A heritable and as yet incurable neurodegenerative disease, characterized by involuntary jerking movements especially in the face, tongue, neck, shoulders, arms and legs; irritability, depression and dementia; usual onset between the ages of 30 and 40. Caused by a *dominant gene* located on chromosome 4.

Hyperactivity   Unusually high activity level that is difficult for an individual to control.

Hypotonia   Reduced tension, such as in the muscles.

Identity   An individual's sense of who he or she is, as well as of affiliation with larger and smaller social groups and communities.

Imitation   The deliberate execution of an action to create a correspondence between what oneself does and what someone else does.

Imprinting   A form of rapid learning that takes place during a short and sensitive period immediately after birth; ducklings, for example, will follow the first person, animal or object they see move within a period of 48 hours after hatching.

Incidence   The appearance of new occurrences of a trait, disease or similar in a particular *population* during a particular time span, often expressed as the number of incidences per 1,000 individuals per year; see *prevalence*.

Individual differences   Variation in skills and characteristics between the individuals in a *population*; see *atypical development* and *typical development*.

Individualistic culture   Society where values emphasize on the uniqueness of each individual; see *collectivist culture*.

Infancy   The first year of life.

Inhibition   Shyness and withdrawal from social challenges.

Integration (in development)   Coordination; progress toward greater organization and a more complex structure.

Intellectual disability; Learning disability; Mental retardation Significant problems learning and adjusting that affect most areas of functioning; graded mild (IQ 70–50), moderate (IQ 49–35), severe (IQ 34–20) and profound (IQ below 20); in clinical contexts, a significant reduction in social adjustment is an additional criterion.

Intelligence quotient (IQ)   Numerical representation of an individual's *intelligence* in relation to peers. Formerly, IQ was based on the relationship between mental age and chronological age, calculated by dividing the *age score* on an IQ test by the individual's chronological age; today, IQ tests are based on a *standard score* with a mean of 100 and a *standard deviation* of 15 or 16, depending on the *test* being used.

Interaction effect   An influence by one or several other factors; see *main effect*.

Klinefelter syndrome   Chromosomal disorder caused by an additional X chromosome in males (XXY); symptoms include sterility, small testes, and long arms and legs; see *sex chromosomes*.

Language function   The purpose of speech; the objective one wants to achieve by conveying something to another person using language.

Learning   Relatively permanent change in understanding and behavior as the result of experience; see *development* and *maturation*.

Learning disorder   Significant problems developing skills in a specific area of knowledge, such as language impairment, reading/ writing disorders (*dyslexia*) and difficulties with math (dyscalculia); often referred to as specific learning disorder as opposed to general learning disability; see *intellectual disability*.

Long-term memory   Part of the memory system that stores memories over time and contains most of an individual's knowledge.

Longitudinal study   Research method that involves the observation of the same individuals at various age levels.

Magnetic resonance imaging, MRI   Method of studying the brain that yields black-and-white images of the brain's shape and size. MRI is sensitive to the cell differences in various tissue types, such as white and gray brain matter.

Main effect   An influence that is independent of other factors; see *interaction effect.*

Maturation   Developmental change caused by genetically determined regulating mechanisms that are relatively independent of the individual's specific experiences; see *development* and *learning.*

Mental disorder   Behavioral or psychological pattern that occurs in an individual and leads to clinically significant distress or impairment in one or more important areas of functioning.

Mirror neuron   Nerve cell that is activated both when an individual observes an action and when he or she performs the action.

Module (in cognition)   Isolated brain system that deals with a particular type of stimulation and knowledge.

Monozygotic twins; Identical twins   Twins resulting from the splitting of the same fertilized egg, sharing 100 percent of each other's genes; see *dizygotic twins (fraternal twins).*

Mutation   Sudden change in a gene.

Myelination   The formation of a thin myelin sheath around the nerve fibers, consisting of proteins and fat and leading to an increase in the transmission of nerve impulses.

Nativism   Theoretical assumption that development proceeds according to a plan that in some way is represented genetically, and that experience has little or no effect on the developmental outcome; see *maturation.*

Natural selection   The principle that genetic changes in a species are due to the fact that offspring with characteristics well-adapted to the current environment are most likely to grow up and propagate, and thus pass on those properties to later generations.

Neonatal period   The first month of life.

Neuroimaging   Using technology to create images of the structures and functions of the brain.

Neuroticism   One of the *Big Five personality traits.*

Neurotransmitter   Chemical substance released from an *axon* to a *neuron* that affects the activity of another neuron.

Ontogeny   The developmental history of an individual.

Perception   Knowledge gained through the senses; discernment, selection and processing of sensory input.

Personality   An individual's characteristic tendency to feel, think and act in specific ways.

Personality traits   Summary description of an individual's *personality.*

Phenotype   An individual's observable physical and psychological characteristics; see *genotype*.

Phenylketonuria (PKU)   Hereditary disorder in the production of the enzyme phenylalanine hydroxy lase, leading to elevated levels of phenylalanine in the blood; causes severe mental and physical impairment if left untreated by a dietary regimen.

Plasticity (in development)   The ability of an organism to change and adapt in response to experiences; frequently used in connection with the nervous system; see *constraint*.

Population (in statistics)   The sum total of individuals, objects, events and the like included in a study. Also used to describe a group of individuals with a common measurable attribute, such as children in a certain school grade or young people in cities.

Postnatal   After birth.

Prader-Willi syndrome   Genetic syndrome characterized by short stature, *hypotonia*, an insatiable appetite and often mild learning disabilities; caused by a missing or unexpressed part of chromosome pair 15, inherited from the father; the counterpart to *Angelman syndrome*; see *genomic imprinting*.

Prenatal period   The developmental period before birth.

Prevalence   Relative presence of for example traits, diseases and syndromes in a particular population at a certain time; see *incidence*.

Recessive gene   Gene that is only expressed when present on both *chromosomes* of a pair, one from each parent; see *dominant gene* and *genomic imprinting*.

Recognition   The process of experiencing something in the moment that has been experienced before, such as when children consciously or nonconsciously show that they have seen a particular image before.

Reflex   Unlearned and involuntary response to an external stimulus.

Regression   The relapse into earlier, more primitive or childish ways of functioning.

Rehabilitation   The effort to build up new or previously existing functions and restore opportunities for interaction and quality of life for people with acquired disabilities; see *habilitation*.

Representation (mental)   An individual's mental storage of understanding and knowledge about the world.

Resilience   Attributes that lead to a positive development under difficult childhood conditions, such as children who are biologically or socially at *risk* of aberrant or delayed development; see *vulnerability*.

Rett syndrome   Genetic syndrome that almost exclusively affects girls; characterized by severe *intellectual disability* and motor and language impairment; development is often normal for the first 6–18 months of life, with a consequent decline in functioning. Believed to be mainly caused by a defective control gene (MeCP$_2$) on the X chromosome that fails to switch off other X chromosome genes at the right time; see *genomic imprinting*.

Ribonucleic acid (RNA)   Macromolecular compounds carrying genetic information and responsible for cellular protein synthesis.

Risk   Increased likelihood of a negative developmental outcome; may be linked to biological and environmental factors.

Rooting reflex   *Developmental reflex* elicited when an infant is lightly touched on the cheek and turns the head toward the side being stimulated; usually disappears at 3 months of age.

School age   Age 6–12.

Self-organizing   The emergence or establishment of new structures not driven by external factors.

Self-regulating   The ability to monitor and adapt one's own thoughts, feelings, reactions and actions in order to cope with the requirements, challenges and opportunities of the environment and be able to achieve one's goals; also referred to as self-control.

Sensitive period   Limited period of time when an individual is particularly susceptible to specific forms of positive or negative stimulation and experience; if the stimulation or experience does not take place during the given time period, the individual will still be able to take advantage of, or be impaired by, similar types of stimulation or experience later in life, but to a lesser extent; see *critical period*.

Sex   See *gender*.

Sex chromosomes   Chromosomal pair that determines the sex of an individual and differs between males (XY) and females (XX).

Sex-linked inheritance   Inherited characteristic related to the genes on the *sex chromosomes*.

Socioeconomic status (SES)   Assessment of an individual's economic and social status in society; for children, usually based on information about the parents' education and occupation.

Standard deviation   Measure of the spread of *quantitative* data; indicates the average degree of deviation in the score or numerical value of a variable from the total average.

Synapse   Contact point between the *axon* of a nerve cell and the body of another nerve cell via its *dendrites*; this is where the transmission of impulses occurs.

Synaptic pruning   Selective loss of synapses during the first years of life due to lack of use.

Syndrome   Set of attributes and behavioral characteristics that regularly occur together.

Temperament   A biologically determined pattern of emotional reactivity and regulation unique to an individual; includes the degree of *emotionality*, *irritability* and *activity level*, and reactions to and ability to cope with emotional situations, new impressions and changes.

Teratogens   Substances that can cause damage to the fetus.

Test   Measurement instrument; a collection of questions or tasks that provide a basis for assessing an individual's performance relative to peers or a specific set of criteria.

Transactional model   Developmental model based on mutual interaction between an individual and the environment over time: the environment changes the individual, the individual changes the environment, which in turn changes the individual, and so on.

Trisomy 21   The most common form of *Down syndrome*, caused by an extra chromosome 21.

Turner syndrome   *Chromosomal abnormality* caused by the presence of only a single X chromosome (X0) in females; characterized by a slightly low weight at birth, heart failure, distinctive facial features, short and chubby fingers, short stature, inability to reproduce and *learning disabilities*.

Typical development   Course of development that characterizes the majority of a *population*; see *atypical development* and *individual differences*.

Vulnerability   An individual's susceptibility to be adversely affected by particular conditions or circumstances in the environment; see *resilience* and *risk*.

Williams syndrome   Genetic syndrome characterized by heart defects, distinctive facial features, a short stature, developmental delays in the fetal stage and later, problems thriving during *infancy*, mild or moderate *learning disabilities*, good language abilities compared with other skills, and trusting behavior toward other people.

Zygote   Cell resulting from the fusion of an egg and a sperm cell.

Bibliography

Abdolmaleky, H. M., Thiagalingam, S., & Wilcox, M. (2005). Genetics and epigenetics in major psychiatric disorders: Dilemmas, achievements, applications, and future scope. *American Journal of Pharmacogenomics, 5,* 149–160.

Ackerman, S. (1992). Discovering the brain. Washington, DC: National Academy Press.

Adolphs, R. (2009). The social brain: Neural basis of social knowledge. *Annual Review of Psychology, 60,* 693–716.

Alhusen, J. L. (2008). A literature update on maternal-fetal attachment. *Journal of Obstetric, Gynecological, and Neonatal Nursing, 37,* 315–328.

Amir, R. E., Van den Veyver, I. B., Wan, M., Tran, C. Q., Francke, U., & Zoghbi, H. Y. (1999). Rett syndrome is caused by mutations in X-linked MECP2, encoding methyl-CpG-binding protein 2. *Nature Genetics, 23,* 185–188.

Baillieux, H., De Smet, H. J., Paquier, P- F., De Deyn, P. P., & Mariën, P. (2008). Cerebellar neurocognition: Insights into the bottom of the brain. *Clinical Neurology and Neurosurgery, 110,* 763–773.

Barinaga, M. (1995). Remapping the motor cortex. *Science, 268,* 1696–1698.

Battro, A. M. (2000). Half a brain is enough: The story of Nico. New York, NY: Cambridge University Press.

Bauman, M. L., Kemper, T. L., & Arin, D. M. (1995). Microscopic observations of the brain in Rett syndrome. *Neuropediatrics, 26,* 105–108.

Baumrind, D. (1993). The average expectable environment is not so good. *Child Development, 64,* 1299–1317.

Baumrind, D., Larzelere, R. E., & Owens, E. B. (2010). Effects of preschool parents' power assertive patterns and practices on adolescent development. *Parenting, 10,* 157–201.

Bayley, N. (2006). Bayley Scales of Infant and Toddler Development, Third edition. San Antonio, Texas: Harcourt Assessment.

Becker, J. (2006). Relation of neurological findings on decoupling of brain activity from limb movement to Piagetian ideas on the origin of thought. *Cognitive Development, 21,* 194–198.

Behnke, M., Smith, V. C., & Committee on Substance Abuse (2013). Prenatal substance abuse: Short- and long-term effects on the exposed fetus. *Pediatrics*, *131*, e1009–e1024.

Belsky, J., & de Haan, M. (2011). Parenting and children's brain development: The end of the beginning. *Journal of Child Psychology and Psychiatry*, *52*, 409–428.

Belsky, J., Jonassaint, C., Pluess, M., Stanton, M., Brummett, B., & Williams, R. (2009). Vulnerability genes or plasticity genes? *Molecular Psychiatry*, *14*, 746–754.

Bishop, D. V. M. (2003). Genetic and environmental risks for specific language impairment in children. *International Congress Series*, *1254*, 225–245.

Bishop, D. V. M. (2013). Cerebral asymmetry and language development: Cause, correlate, or consequence? *Science*, *340 (6138)*, 1230531.

Bishop, D. V. M., Nation, K., & Patterson, K. (2014). When words fail us: Insights into language processing from developmental and acquired disorders. *Philosophical Transactions of the Royal Society of London. Series B, Biological Sciences*, *369*, 20120403.

Borgstein, J., & Grootendorst, C. (2002). Half a brain. *The Lancet*, *359 (9305)*, 473.

Bourgeois, J. P. (1997). Synaptogenesis, heterochrony and epigenesis in the mammalian neocortex. *Acta Pædiatrica, Supplement*, *422*, 27–33.

Brodal, P. (2004). The central nervous system: Structure and function. Oxford: Oxford University Press.

Brown, T. T., & Jernigan, T. L. (2012). Brain development during the preschool years. *Neuropsychology Review*, *22*, 313–333.

Bulteau, C., Jambaqué, I., Chiron, C., Rodrigo, S., Dorfmüller, G., Dulac, O., Hertz-Pannier, L., & Noulhiane, M. (2017). Language plasticity after hemispherotomy of the dominant hemisphere in 3 patients: Implication of non-linguistic networks. *Epilepsy and Behavior*, *69*, 86–94.

Butterworth, G., & Harris, M. (1994). Principles of developmental psychology. Hove, UK: Erlbaum.

Caballero, A., Granberg, R., & Tseng, K. Y. (2016). Mechanisms contributing to prefrontal cortex maturation during adolescence. *Neuroscience and Biobehavioral Reviews*, *70*, 4–12.

Caramazza, A., Anzellotti, S., Strnad, L., & Lingnau, A. (2014). Embodied cognition and mirror neurons: A critical assessment. *Annual Review of Neuroscience*, *37*, 1–15.

Casey, B. J., Tottenham, N., Liston, C., & Durston, S. (2005). Imaging the developing brain: What have we learned about cognitive development? *Trends in Cognitive Science*, *9*, 104–110.

Caspi, A., McClay, J., Moffitt, T. E., Mill, J., Martin, J., Craig, I. W., Taylor, A., & Poulton, R. (2002). Role of genotype in the cycle of violence in maltreated children. *Science*, *297*, 851–854.

Chiao, J. Y., Hariri, A. R., Harada, T., Mano, Y., Sadato, N., Parrish, T. B., & Iidaka, T. (2010). Theory and methods in cultural neuroscience. *Social Cognitive and Affective Neuroscience, 5,* 356–361.

Choufani, S., & Weksberg, R. (2016). Genomic imprinting. In D. P. Bazett-Jones & G. Dellaire (Eds), The functional nucleus (pp. 449–465). Switzerland: Springer.

Cicchetti, D. (2002). The impact of social experience on neurobiological systems: Illustration from a constructivist view of child maltreatment. *Cognitive Development, 17,* 1407–1428.

Cnattingius, S. (2004). The epidemiology of smoking during pregnancy: Smoking prevalence, maternal characteristics, and pregnancy outcomes. *Nicotine and Tobacco Research, 6* (Suppl-2), S125–S140.

Cook, R., Bird, G., Catmur, C., Press, C., & Heyes, C. (2014). Mirror neurons: From origin to function. *Behavioral and Brain Sciences, 37,* 177–192.

Couperus, J. W., & Nelson, C. A. (2006). Early brain development and plasticity. In K. McCartney & D. Phillips, (Eds). Blackwell handbook of early childhood development (pp. 85–105). Malden, MA: Blackwell.

Crusio, W. E. (2015). Key issues in contemporary behavioral genetics. *Current Opinion in Behavioral Sciences, 2,* 89–95.

Darwin, C. (1859). On the origin of species by means of natural selection or the preservation of favored races in the struggle for life. London: Murray.

Davies, J. R., Dent, C. L., McNamara, G. I., & Isles, A. R. (2015). Behavioural effects of imprinted genes. *Current Opinion in Behavioral Sciences, 2,* 28–33.

Dawson, G. (1994). Development of emotional expression and emotion regulation in infancy: Contributions of the frontal lobe. In G. Dawson & K. W. Fischer (Eds), Human behavior and the developing brain (pp. 346–379). New York, NY: Guilford Press.

de Colibus, L., Li, M., Binda, C., Edmondson, D. E., & Mattevi, A. (2005). *Proceedings of the National Academy of Science in United States of America, 102,* 2684–12689.

de Haan, M., & Johnson, M. (2003). Mechanisms and theories of brain development. In M. de Haan & M. Johnson (Eds), The cognitive neuroscience of development (pp. 1–18). Hove, UK: Psychology Press.

De Santis, M., Cavaliere, A. F., Straface, G., & Caruso, A. (2006). Rubella infection in pregnancy. *Reproductive Toxicology, 21,* 390–398.

de Vries, J. I. P., Visser, G. H. A., & Prechtl, H. F. R. (1982). The emergence of fetal behavior: I. Qualitative aspects. *Early Human Development, 7,* 301–322.

de Vries, J. I. P., Visser, G. H. A., & Prechtl, H. F. R. (1985). The emergence of fetal behaviour: II. Quantitative aspects. *Early Human Development, 12,* 99–120.

de Vries, J. I. P., Visser, G. H. A., & Prechtl, H. F. R. (1988). The emergence of fetal behaviour: III. Individual differences and consistencies. *Early Human Development, 16,* 85–103.

Dekker, T. M., & Karmiloff-Smith, A. (2011). The dynamics of ontogeny: A neuroconstructivist perspective on genes, brains, cognition and behavior. *Progress in Brain Research, 189,* 23–33.

Dennis, E. L., & Thompson, P. M. (2013). Typical and atypical brain development: A review of neuroimaging studies. *Dialogues in Clinical Neuroscience, 15,* 359–384.

Di Martino, A., Fair, D. A., Kelly, C., Satterthwaite, T. D., Castellanos, F. X., Thomason, M. E., Craddock, R. C., Luna, B., Leventhal, B. L., Zuo, X. N., et al. (2014). Unraveling the miswired connectome: A developmental perspective. *Neuron, 83,* 1335–1353.

DiPietro, J. A. (2010). Psychological and psychophysiological considerations regarding the maternal–fetal relationship. *Infant and Child Development, 19,* 27–38.

Drillien, C. M., & Wilkinson, E. M. (1964). Emotional stress and mongoloid births. *Developmental Medicine and Child Neurology, 6,* 140–143.

Ehrhart, F., Coort, S. L., Cirillo, E., Smeets, E., Evelo, C. T., & Curfs, L. M. (2016). Rett syndrome–biological pathways leading from MECP2 to disorder phenotypes. *Orphanet Journal of Rare Diseases, 11,* 158.

Ellison, P. T. (2010). Fetal programming and fetal psychology. *Infant and Child Development, 19,* 6–20.

Elman, J. L. (2005). Connections models of development: Where next? *Trends in Cognitive Science, 9,* 111–117.

Evrard, P., Marret, S., & Gressens, P. (1997). Environmental and genetic determinant of neural migration and post-migratory survival. *Acta Pædiatrica, Supplement, 422,* 20–26.

Faraone, S. V., Smoller, J. W., Pato, C. N., Sullivan, P., & Tsuang, M. T. (2008). The new neuropsychiatric genetics. *American Journal of Medical Genetics Part B: Neuropsychiatric Genetics, 147,* 1–2.

Field, T. (2011). Prenatal depression effects on early development: A review. *Infant Behavior and Development, 34,* 1–14.

Fifer, W. P., Monk, C. E., & Grose-Fifer, J. (2004). Prenatal development and risk. In G. Bremner & A. Fogel (Eds), Blackwell handbook of infant development (pp. 505–542). Malden, MA: Blackwell.

Finne, P. H., Seip, M., & Salomonsen, L. (2001). Propedeutisk pediatri. Oslo: Universitetsforlaget.

Flynn, J. R. (2016). Does your family make you smarter? Nature, nurture and human autonomy. Cambridge: Cambridge University Press.

Fogassi, L., & Ferrari, P. F. (2011). Mirror systems. *WIREs Cognitive Science, 2,* 22–38.

Foley, D. L., Eaves, L. J., Wormley, B., Silberg, J. L., Maes, H. H., Kuhn, J., & Riley, B. (2004). Childhood adversity, monoamine oxidase a genotype, and risk for conduct disorder. *Archives of General Psychiatry, 61,* 738–744.

Gagnon, R. (1992). Fetal behaviour in relation to stimulation. In J. G. Nijhuis (Ed.), Fetal behavior (pp. 209–226). Oxford: Oxford Medical Publications.

Gallese, V., Fadiga, L., Fogassi, L., & Rizzolatti, G. (1996). Action recognition in the premotor cortex. *Brain. 119*, 593–609.

Gapp, K., Woldemichael, B. T., Bohacek, J., & Mansuy, I. M. (2014). Epigenetic regulation in neurodevelopment and neurodegenerative diseases. *Neuroscience, 264*, 99–111.

Gee, D. G., Gabard-Durnam, L. J., Flannery, J., Goff, B., Humphreys, K. L., Telzer, E. H., Hare, T. A., Bookheimer, S. Y., & Tottenham, N. (2013). Early developmental emergence of human amygdala–prefrontal connectivity after maternal deprivation. *Proceedings of the National Academy of Sciences, 110*, 15638–15643.

Gerstein, M. B., Bruce, C., Rozowsky, J. S., Zheng, D., Du, J., Korbel. J. O., Emanuelsson, O., Zhang, Z. D., Weissman, S., & Snyder, M. (2007). What is a gene, post-ENCODE? History and updated definition. *Genome Research, 17*, 669–681.

Geschwind, D. H. (2011). Genetics of autism spectrum disorders. *Trends in Cognitive Sciences, 15*, 409–416.

Geschwind, D. H., & Flint, J. (2015). Genetics and genomics of psychiatric disease. *Science, 349 (6255)*, 1489–1494.

Geschwind, N., & Galaburda, A. M. (1985). Cerebral lateralization: Biological mechanisms, associations, and pathology: I. A hypothesis and a program for research. *Archives of Neurology, 42*, 428–459.

Gluckman, P. D., & Hanson, M. A. (2010). The plastic human. *Infant and Child Development, 19*, 21–26.

Gottesman, I. I., & Hanson, D. R. (2005). Human development: Biological and genetic processes. *Annual Review of Psychology, 56*, 263–286.

Gottlieb, G. (1992). Individual development and evolution. Oxford: Oxford University Press.

Gottlieb, G. (1995). Some conceptual deficiencies in "developmental" behavior genetics. *Human Development, 38*, 131–141.

Gottlieb, G. (2002). Developmental-behavioral initiation of evolutionary change. *Psychological Review, 109*, 211–218.

Gottlieb, G. (2007). Probabilistic epigenesis. *Developmental Science, 10*, 1–11.

Gottlieb, G., Wahlsten, D., & Lickliter, R. (2006). The significance of biology for human development: A developmental psychobiological systems view. In R. W. Damon & R. M. Lerner (Eds), Handbook of child development, Sixth edition, Volume 1: Theoretical models of human development (pp. 210–257). New York, NY: Wiley.

Grayson, D. S., & Fair, D. A. (2017). Development of large-scale functional networks from birth to adulthood: A guide to the neuroimaging literature. *NeuroImage, 160*, 15–31.

Grossman, S. W., Churchill, J. D., McKinney, B. C., Kodish, I. M., Otte, S. L., & Greenough, W. T. (2003). Experience effects on brain development: Possible contributions to psychopathology. *Journal of Child Psychology and Psychiatry, 44*, 33–63.

Guerrini, I., Thomson, A. D., & Gurling, H. D. (2007). The importance of alcohol misuse, malnutrition and genetic susceptibility on brain growth and plasticity. *Neuroscience and Biobehavioral Reviews, 31*, 212–220.

Gutteling, B. M., de Weerth, C., Willemsen-Swinkels, S. H. N., Huizink, A. C., Mulder, E. J. H., Visser, G. H. A., & Buitelaar, J. K. (2005). The effects of prenatal stress on temperament and problem behavior of 27-month-old toddlers. *European Child and Adolescent Psychiatry, 14*, 41–51.

Gutteling, B. M., de Weerth, C., Zandbelt, N., Mulder, E. J., Visser, G. H., & Buitelaar, J. K., (2006). Does maternal prenatal stress adversely affect the child's learning and memory at age six? *Journal of Abnormal Child Psychology, 34*, 789–798.

Guyer, A. E., Silk, J. S., & Nelson, E. E. (2016). The neurobiology of the emotional adolescent: From the inside out. *Neuroscience and Biobehavioral Reviews, 70*, 74–85.

Haak, K. V., Langers, D. R., Renken, R., van Dijk, P., Borgstein, J., & Cornelissen, F. W. (2014). Abnormal visual field maps in human cortex: A mini-review and a case report. *Cortex, 56*, 14–25.

Hales, C. N., & Barker, D. J. (2001). The thrifty phenotype hypothesis. *British Medical Bulletin, 60*, 5–20.

Hari, R., & Kujala, M. (2009). Brain basis of human social interaction: From concepts to brain imaging. *Physiological Reviews, 89*, 453–479.

Hassold, T., & Sherman, S. (2000). Down syndrome: Genetic recombination and the origin of the extra chromosome 21. *Clinical Genetics, 57*, 95–100.

Heard, E., & Martienssen, R. A. (2014). Transgenerational epigenetic inheritance: Myths and mechanisms. *Cell, 157*, 95–109.

Hepper, P. G. (1992). Fetal psychology: An embryonic science. In J. G. Nijhuis (Ed.), Fetal behavior (pp. 129–156). Oxford: Oxford Medical Publications.

Hepper, P. G. (2015). Behavior during the prenatal period: Adaptive for development and survival. *Child Development Perspectives, 9*, 38–43.

Hepper, P. G. (2016). Observing the fetus' behavior to assess health: The behavior of the human fetus in response to maternal alcohol consumption. In N. Reissland & B. S. Kisilevsky (Eds), Fetal development (pp. 317–330). Cham, Switzerland: Springer.

Hickok, G. (2013). Do mirror neurons subserve action understanding? *Neuroscience Letters, 540*, 56–58.

Hilgetag, C. C., & Barbas, H. (2009). Sculpting the brain. *Scientific American, 300*, 66–71.

Hodapp, R. M. (1997). Direct and indirect behavioral effects of different genetic disorders of mental retardation. *American Journal on Mental Retardation, 102*, 67–79.

Horwitz, B., & Horovitz, S. G. (2012). Introduction to research topic–brain connectivity analysis: Investigating brain disorders. Part 1: The review articles. *Frontiers in Systems Neuroscience, 6*, 3.

Howe, M. J. A., Davidson, J. W., & Sloboda, J. A. (1998). Innate talents: Reality or myth? *Behavioral and Brain Sciences, 21*, 399–407.

Hudziak, J. J., & Faraone, S. V. (2010). The new genetics in child psychiatry. *Journal of the American Academy of Child and Adolescent Psychiatry, 49*, 729–735.

Hunt, R. H., & Thomas, K. M. (2008). Magnetic resonance imaging methods in developmental science: A primer. *Development and Psychopathology, 20*, 1029–1051.

Hunter, S., Hurley, R. A., & Taber, K. H. (2013). A look inside the mirror neuron system. *The Journal of Neuro psychiatry and Clinical Neurosciences, 25*, 170–175.

Huttenlocher, P. R. (1990). Morphometric study of human cerebral cortex development. *Neuropsychologia, 28*, 517–527.

Hyde, L. W. (2015). Developmental psychopathology in an era of molecular genetics and neuroimaging: A developmental neurogenetics approach. *Development and Psychopathology, 27*, 587–613.

Immordino-Yang, M. H. (2007). Compensation after losing half of the brain. In A. Nava, (Ed.), Critical issues in brain science and pedagogy (pp. 45–54) San Francisco, CA: McGraw Hill.

Irner, T. B. (2012). Substance exposure in utero and developmental consequences in adolescence: A systematic review, *Child Neuropsychology, 18*, 521–549.

Jacob, P. (2009). The tuning-fork model of human social cognition: A critique. *Consciousness and Cognition, 18*, 229–243.

Jacob, P. (2013). How from action-mirroring to intention-ascription? *Consciousness and Cognition, 22*, 1132–1141.

James, D. K. (2010). Fetal learning: A critical review. *Infant and Child Development, 19*, 45–54.

Jiang, Y., Guo, X., Zhang, J., Gao, J., Wang, X., Situ, W., Yi, J., Zhang, X., Zhu, X., Yao, S., & Huang, B. (2015). Abnormalities of cortical structures in adolescent onset conduct disorder. *Psychological Medicine, 45*, 3467–3479.

Johnson, M. H. (1998). The neural basis of cognitive development. In W. Damon, D. Kuhn & R. S. Siegler (Eds), Handbook of child psychology, Fifth edition, Volume 2: Cognition, perception and language (pp. 1–49). New York, NY: Wiley.

Johnson, M. H. (2011). Interactive specialization: A domain-general framework for human functional brain development? *Developmental Cognitive Neuroscience, 1*, 7–21.

Johnson, M. H., Grossmann, T., & Cohen Kadosh, K. (2009). Mapping functional brain development: Building a social brain through interactive specialization. *Developmental Psychology, 45*, 151–159.

Johnson, M. H., Halit, H., Grice, S. J. & Karmiloff-Smith, A. (2002). Neuroimaging of typical and atypical development: A perspective from multiple levels of analysis. *Development and Psychopathology, 14*, 521–536.

Joseph, J. (2013). The use of the classical twin method in the social and behavioral sciences: The fallacy continues. *The Journal of Mind and Behavior, 34*, 1–39.

Joseph, R. (2000). Fetal brain behavior and cognitive development. *Developmental Review, 21*, 81–98.

Kagan, J. (2007). What is emotion? New Haven, CT: Yale University Press.

Kagan, J. (2009). The three cultures: Natural sciences, social sciences, and the humanities in the 21st century. Cambridge: Cambridge University Press.

Kana, R. K., Uddin, L. Q., Kenet, T., Chugani, D., & Müller, R. A. (2014). Brain connectivity in autism. *Frontiers in Human Neuroscience, 8*, 349.

Kang, C., & Drayna, D. (2011). Genetics of speech and language disorders. *Annual Review of Genomics and Human Genetics, 12*, 145–164.

Karmiloff-Smith, A. (1998). Development itself is the key to understanding developmental disorders. *Trends in Cognitive Sciences, 2*, 389–398.

Karmiloff-Smith, A. (2009). Nativism versus neuroconstructivism: Rethinking the study of developmental disorders. *Developmental Psychology, 45*, 56–63.

Karmiloff-Smith, A. (2010). A developmental perspective on modularity. In B. Glatzeder, V. Goel & A. Müller (Eds), Towards a theory of thinking on thinking, Part 3 (pp. 179–187). Berlin: Springer.

Karmiloff-Smith, A. (2011). Static snapshots versus dynamic approaches to genes, brain, cognition and behaviour in neurodevelopmental disabilities. *International Review of Research in Developmental Disabilities, 40*, 1–16.

Keil, F. C. (1990). Constraints on constraints: Surveying the epigenetic landscape. *Cognitive Science, 14*, 135–168.

Khundrakpam, B. S., Reid, A., Brauer, J., Carbonell, F., Lewis, J., Ameis, S., et al. (2013). Developmental changes in organization of structural brain networks. *Cerebral Cortex, 23*, 2072–2085.

Kim-Cohen, J., Caspi, A., Taylor, A., Williams, B., Newcombe, R., Craig, I., & Moffitt, T. E. (2006). MAOA, maltreatment, and gene-environment interaction predicting children's mental health: New evidence and a meta-analysis. *Molecular Psychiatry, 11*, 903–913.

Kisilevsky, B. S. (2016). Fetal auditory processing: Implications for language development? In N. Reissland & B. S. Kisilevsky (Eds), Fetal development (pp. 133–152). Cham, Switzerland: Springer.

Kisilevsky, B. S., Chambers, B., Parker, K., & Davies, G. A. L. (2014). Auditory processing in growth restricted fetuses and newborns and later language development. *Clinical Psychological Science, 2*, 495–513.

Kisilevsky, B. S., Hains, S. M. J., Brown, C. A., Lee, C. T., Cowperthwaite, B., Stutzman, S. S., Swansburg, M. L., Lee, K., Xie, X., Huang, H., et al. (2009). Foetal sensitivity to properties of maternal speech and language. *Infant Behavior and Development, 32*, 59–71.

Kleefstra, T., Schencka, A., Kramera, J. M., & van Bokhove, H. (2014). The genetics of cognitive epigenetics. *Neuropharmacology, 80*, 83–94.

Kolb, B., Mychasiuk, R., Muhammad, A., & Gibb, R. (2013). Brain plasticity in the developing brain. *Progress in Brain Research, 207*, 35–64.

Konrad, K., Firk, C., & Uhlhaas, P. J. (2013). Brain development during adolescence: Neuroscientific insights into this developmental period. *Deutsches Ärzteblatt International, 110*, 425–431.

Kopsida, E., Mikaelsson, M. A., & Davies, W. (2011). The role of imprinted genes in mediating susceptibility to neuropsychiatric disorders. *Hormones and Behavior, 59*, 375–382.

Lai, C. S. L., Fisher, S. E., Hurst, J. A., Vargha-Khadem, F., & Monaco, A. P. (2001). A forkhead-domain gene is mutated in a severe speech and language disorder. *Nature, 413*, 519–523.

Lamarck, J. B. P. (1809). Philosophie zoologique. Paris: L'Imprimerie de Duminil-Lesueur.

Landerl, K., & Moll, K. (2010). Comorbidity of learning disorders: Prevalence and familial transmission. *Journal of Child Psychology and Psychiatry, 51*, 287–294.

Latham, J., & Wilson, A. (2010). The great DNA data deficit: Are genes for disease a mirage? *The Bioscience Research Project*, 18–21.

Lazinski, M. J., Shea, A. K., & Steiner, M. (2008). Effects of maternal prenatal stress on offspring development: A commentary. *Archives of Women's Mental Health, 11*, 363–375.

Leader, L. R. (1995). The potential value of habituation in the neonate. In J.-P. Lecanuet, W. P. Fifer, N. A. Krasnegor & W. P. Smotherman (Eds), Fetal development (pp. 383–404). Hove, UK: Lawrence Erlbaum.

Leader, L. R. (2016). The potential value of habituation in the fetus. In N. Reissland & B. S. Kisilevsky (Eds), Fetal development (pp. 189–209). Cham, Switzerland: Springer.

Lecanuet, J.-P., & Schaal, B. (2002). Sensory performances in the human foetus: A brief summary of research. *Intellectica, 34*, 29–56.

Lenroot, R. K., & Giedd, J. N. (2008). The changing impact of genes and environment on brain development during childhood and adolescence: Initial findings from a neuroimaging study of pediatric twins. *Developmental Psychopathology, 20*, 1161–1175.

Lerner, R. M. (2015). Eliminating genetic reductionism from developmental science. *Research in Human Development, 12*, 178–188.

Lewis, M. (2005). Self-organizing individual differences in brain development. *Developmental Review, 25*, 252–277.

Liao, X., Vasilakos, A. V., & He, Y. (2017). Small-world human brain networks: Perspectives and challenges. *Neuroscience and Biobehavioral Reviews, 77*, 286–300.

Little, C. M. (2011). Genetics and twins. *Newborn and Infant Nursing Reviews, 11*, 185–189.

Lyall, A. E., Shi, F., Geng, X., Woolson, S., Li, G., Wang, L., Hamer, R. M., Shen, D., & Gilmore, J. H. (2015). Dynamic development of regional cortical thickness and surface area in early childhood. *Cerebral Cortex, 25*, 2204–2212.

Lyst, M. J., & Bird, A. (2015). Rett syndrome: A complex disorder with simple roots. *Nature Reviews Genetics, 16*, 261–275.

Mahy, C. E., Moses, L. J., & Pfeifer, J. H. (2014). How and where: Theory-of-mind in the brain. *Developmental Cognitive Neuroscience, 9,* 68–81.

Manuck, S. B., & McCaffery, J. M. (2014). Gene-environment interaction. *Annual Review of Psychology, 65,* 41–70.

Mareschal, D., Johnson, M. H., Sirois, S., Spratling, M., Thomas, M., & Westermann, G. (2007a). Neuroconstructivism, Volume I. How the brain constructs cognition. Oxford: Oxford University Press.

Mareschal, D., Sirois, S., Westermann, G., & Johnson, M. H. (2007b). Neuroconstructivism, Volume II. Perspectives and prospects. Oxford: Oxford University Press.

Mari, F., Kilstrup-Nielsen, C., Cambi, F., Speciale, C., Mencarelli, M. A., & Renieri, A. (2005). Genetics and mechanisms of disease in Rett syndrome. *Drug Discovery Today: Disease Mechanisms, 2,* 419–425.

Marshall, P. J. (2016). Embodiment and human development. *Child Development Perspectives, 10,* 245–250.

McCartney, K., Harris, M. J., & Bernieri, F. (1990). Growing up and growing apart: A developmental meta-analysis of twin studies. *Psychological Bulletin, 107,* 226–237.

McCorry, N. K., & Hepper, P. G. (2007). Fetal habituation performance: Gestational age and sex effects. *British Journal of Developmental Psychology, 25,* 277–292.

McGowan, P. O., & Szyf, M. (2010). The epigenetics of social adversity in early life: Implications for mental health outcomes. *Neurobiology of Disease, 39,* 66–72.

McIntosh, G. C., Olshan, A. F., & Baird, P. A. (1995). Paternal age and the risk of birth-defects in offspring. *Epidemiology, 6,* 282–288.

McMahon, E., Wintermark, P., & Lahav, A. (2012). Auditory brain development in premature infants: The importance of early experience. *Annals of the New York Academy of Sciences, 1252,* 17–24.

Meissner, W. W. (2008). Mind-brain and consciousness in psychoanalysis. *Bulletin of the Menninger Clinic, 72,* 283–312.

Menon, V. (2013). Developmental pathways to functional brain networks: Emerging principles. *Trends in Cognitive Sciences, 17,* 627–640.

Millan, M. J. (2013). An epigenetic framework for neurodevelopmental disorders: From pathogenesis to potential therapy. *Neuropharmacology, 68,* 2–82.

Miller, G. A. (2010). Mistreating psychology in the Decade of the Brain. *Perspectives on Psychological Science, 5,* 716–743.

Mills, K. L. (2015). Social development in adolescence: Brain and behavioural changes. Doctoral dissertation, University College London.

Monk, C., Spicer, J., & Champagne, F. A. (2012). Linking prenatal maternal adversity to developmental outcomes in infants: The role of epigenetic pathways. *Development and Psychopathology, 24,* 1361–1376.

Moore, K. L., & Persaud, T. V. N. (2008). The developing human brain, Eighth edition. Philadelphia, PA: W. B. Saunders.

Mulder, E. J. H., de Medina, P. G. R., Huizink, A. C., Van den Bergh, B. R. H., Buitelaar, J. K., & Visser, G. H. A. (2002). Prenatal maternal stress: Effects on pregnancy and the (unborn) child. *Early Human Development, 70,* 3–14.

Mulder, E. J. H., & Visser, G. H. (2016). Fetal behavior: Clinical and experimental research in the human. In N. Reissland & B. S. Kisilevsky (Eds), Fetal development (pp. 87–105). Cham, Switzerland: Springer.

Mund, M., Louwen, F., Klingelhoefer, D., & Gerber, A. (2013). Smoking and pregnancy – a review on the first major environmental risk factor of the unborn. *International Journal of Environmental Research and Public Health, 10,* 6485–6499.

Näätänen, R. (2003). Mismatch negativity: Clinical research and possible applications. *International Journal of Psychophysiology, 48,* 179–188.

Nahum, M., Lee, H., & Merzenich, M. M. (2013). Principles of neuroplasticity-based rehabilitation. *Progress in Brain Research, 207,* 141–171.

Nelson, C. A., & Bosquet, M. (2000). Neurobiology of fetal and infant development: Implications for infant mental health. In C. H. Zeanah (Ed.), Handbook of infant mental health, Second edition (pp. 37–59). New York, NY: Guilford Press.

Nelson, C. A., Thomas, K. M., & de Haan, M. (2006b). Neural bases of cognitive development. In W. Damon, R. M. Lerner, D. Kuhn, R. & S. Siegler (Eds), Handbook of child psychology, Sixth edition, Volume 2: Cognition perception, and language (pp. 3–57). Hoboken, NJ: Wiley.

Neubauer, S., & Hublin, J. J. (2012). The evolution of human brain development. *Evolutionary Biology, 39,* 568–586.

Newbury, D. F., Bonora, E., Lamb, J. A., Fisher, S. E., Lai, C. S., Baird, G., Jannoun, L., Slonims, V., Stott, C. M., Merricks, M. J., et al. (2002). FOXP2 is not a major susceptibility gene for autism or specific language impairment. *The American Journal of Human Genetics, 70,* 1318–1327.

O'Donnell, K. J., Glover, V., Barker, E. D., & O'Connor, T. G. (2014). The persisting effect of maternal mood in pregnancy on childhood psychopathology. *Developmental Psychopathology, 26,* 393–403.

O'Leary, C. M., & Bower, C. (2012). Guidelines for pregnancy: What's an acceptable risk, and how is the evidence (finally) shaping up? *Drug and Alcohol Review, 31,* 170–183.

Owen, A. M., Hampshire, A., Grahn, J. A., Stenton, R., Dajani, S., Burns, A. S., Howard, R. J., & Ballard, C. G. (2010). Putting brain training to the test. *Nature, 465 (7299),* 775–779.

Pennington, B. F. (2015). Atypical cognitive development. In R. M. Lerner, L. S. Liben & U. Mueller (Eds), Handbook of child psychology and developmental science, Seventh edition, Volume 2: Cognitive processes (pp. 995–1037). New York, NY: Wiley.

Perez, J. D., Rubinstein, N. D., & Dulac, C. (2016). New perspectives on genomic imprinting, an essential and multifaceted mode of epigenetic control in the developing and adult brain. *Annual Review of Neuroscience, 39,* 347–384.

Persico, A. M., & Napolioni, V. (2013). Autism genetics. *Behavioural Brain Research, 251,* 95–112.

Pessoa, L., & Adolphs, R. (2010). Emotion processing and the amygdala: From a "low road" to "many roads" of evaluating biological significance. *Nature Reviews Neuroscience, 11,* 773.

Picton, T. W., & Taylor, M. J. (2007). Electrophysiological evaluation of human brain development. *Developmental Neuropsychology, 31,* 249–278.

Pillai, M., & James, D. (1990). Development of human fetal behavior: A review. *Fetal Diagnosis and Therapy, 5,* 15–32.

Pinker, S., & Jackendoff, R. (2005). The faculty of language: What's special about it? *Cognition, 95,* 201–236.

Piontelli, A., Ceriani, F., Fabietti, I., Fogliani, R., Restelli, E., & Kustermann, A. (2015). Fetal sensory abilities. In A. Piontelli (Ed.), Development of normal fetal movements (pp. 111–126). Milan: Springer.

Plomin, R., Corley, R., Caspi, A., Fulker, D. W., & DeFries, J. (1998). Adoption results for self-reported personality: Evidence for nonadditive genetic effects? *Journal of Personality and Social Psychology, 75,* 211–218.

Plomin, R., DeFries, J. C., McClearn, G. E., & McGuffin, P. (2008). Behavioral genetics, Fifth edition. New York, NY: Worth.

Plomin, R., DeFries, J. C., McClearn, G. E., & Rutter, M. (1997). Behavioral genetics, Third edition. New York, NY: W. H. Freeman.

Plomin, R., Haworth, C. M., Meaburn, E. L., Price, T. S., Wellcome Trust Case Control Consortium 2, & Davis, O. S. (2013). Common DNA markers can account for more than half of the genetic influence on cognitive abilities. *Psychological Science, 24,* 562–568.

Pluess, M., & Belsky, J. (2010). Differential susceptibility to parenting and quality child care. *Developmental Psychology, 46,* 379–390.

Pluess, M., & Belsky, J. (2011). Prenatal programming of postnatal plasticity? *Development and Psychopathology, 23,* 29–38.

Poldrack, R. A. (2010). Interpreting developmental changes in neuroimaging signals. *Human Brain Mapping, 31,* 872–878.

Preyer, W. (1882/1988). The mind of the child. New York, NY: Appleton.

Querleu, D., Renard, X., Versyp, F., Paris-Delrue, L., & Crépin, G. (1988). Fetal hearing. *European Journal of Obstetrics and Reproductive Biology, 29,* 191–212.

Rabipour, S., & Raz, A. (2012). Training the brain: Fact and fad in cognitive and behavioral remediation. *Brain and Cognition, 79,* 159–179.

Rakic, P., Bourgeois, J. P., Eckenhoff, M. F., Zecevic, N., & Goldman-Rakic, P. S. (1986). Concurrent overproduction of synapses in diverse regions of the primate cerebral cortex. *Science, 232,* 232–235.

Reissland, N., & Kisilevsky, B. S. (Eds) (2016). Fetal development: Research on brain and behavior, environmental influences, and emerging technologies. Cham, Switzerland: Springer.

Riley, E. P., Infante, M. A., & Warren, K. R. (2011). Fetal alcohol spectrum disorders: An overview. *Neuropsychology Review, 21,* 73.

Rizzolatti, G., & Sinigaglia, C. (2010). The functional role of the parieto-frontal mirror circuit: Interpretations and misinterpretations. *Nature Review Neuroscience*, *11*, 264–274.

Robinson, M., Mattes, E., Oddy, W. H., Pennell, C. E., van Eekelen, A., McLean, N. J., Jacoby, P., Li, J., De Klerk, N. H., Zubrick, S. R., et al. (2011). Prenatal stress and risk of behavioral morbidity from age 2 to 14 years: The influence of the number, type, and timing of stressful life events. *Development and Psychopathology*, *23*, 507–520.

Ronca, A. E., & Alberts, J. R. (1995). Maternal contributions to fetal experience and the transition from prenatal to postnatal life. In J.-P. Lecanuet, W. P. Fifer, N. A. Krasnegor & W. P. Smotherman (Eds), Fetal development (pp. 331–350). Hove, UK: Lawrence Erlbaum.

Ronca, A. E., & Alberts, J. R. (2016). Fetal and birth experiences: Proximate effects, developmental consequences, epigenetic legacies. In N. Reissland & B. S. Kisilevsky (Eds), Fetal development (pp. 15–42). Cham, Switzerland: Springer.

Rose, S. P. R. (1997). Rise of neurogenetic determinism. *Acta Pædiatrica, Supplement86*, 38–40.

Rutter, M. (2006). Genes and behavior: Nature–nurture interplay explained. Oxford: Blackwell.

Rutter, M. (2014). Nature-nurture integration. In M. Lewis & K. Rudolph (Eds), Handbook of developmental psychopathology, Third edition (pp. 45–65). New York, NY: Springer.

Sameroff, A. J. (2010). A unified theory of development: A dialectic integration of nature and nurture. *Child Development*, *81*, 6–22.

Scarr, S. (1992). Developmental theories for the 1990s: Development and individual differences. *Child Development*, *63*, 1–19.

Scarr, S. (1996). How people make their own environments: Implications for parents and policy makers. *Psychology, Public Policy, and Law*, *2*, 204–228.

Schaal, B., Orgeur, P., & Rognon, C. (1995). Odor sensing in the human fetus: Anatomical, functional, and chemoecological bases. In J.-P. Lecanuet, W. P. Fifer, N. A. Krasnegor & W. P. Smotherman (Eds), Fetal development (pp. 205–237). Hove, UK: Erlbaum.

Schrott, L. M. (1997). Effect of training and environment on brain morphology and behavior. *Acta Pædiatrica, Supplement*, *422*, 45–47.

Singer, E. (2013). Play and playfulness, basic features of early childhood education. *European Early Childhood Education Research Journal*, *21*, 172–184.

Sirois, S., Spratling, M., Thomas, M. S., Westermann, G., Mareschal, D., & Johnson, M. H. (2008). Precis of neuroconstructivism: How the brain constructs cognition. *Behavior and Brain Science*, *31*, *321–331*, Discussion, 331–356.

Spinath, F. M., Price, T. S., Dale, P. S., & Plomin, R. (2004). The genetic and environmental origins of language disability and ability. *Child Development*, *75*, 445–454.

Steinhorst, A., & Funke, J. (2014). Mirror neuron activity is no proof for action understanding. *Frontiers in Human Neuroscience, 8*, 333.

Stiles, J., Brown, T. T., Haist, F., & Jernigan, T. (2015). Brain and cognitive development. In R. M. Lerner, L. S. Liben & U. Mueller (Eds), Handbook of child psychology and developmental science, Seventh edition, Volume 2: Cognitive processes (pp. 9–62). Hoboken, NJ: Wiley.

Stott, D. H. (1973). Follow-up study from birth of the effects of prenatal stresses. *Developmental Medicine and Child Neurology, 15*, 770–787.

Swaney, W. T. (2011). Genomic imprinting and mammalian reproduction. *Hormones and Behavior, 59*, 369–374.

Tammen, S. A., Friso, S., & Choi, S. W. (2013). Epigenetics: The link between nature and nurture. *Molecular Aspects of Medicine, 34*, 753–764.

Thomas, M. S., Davis, R., Karmiloff-Smith, A., Knowland, V. C., & Charman, T. (2016). The over-pruning hypothesis of autism. *Developmental Science, 19*, 284–305.

Thomas, M. S. C., Purser, H. R. M., & Richardson, F. M. (2013). Modularity and developmental disorders. In P. D. Zelazo (Ed.), Oxford handbook of developmental psychology (pp. 481–505). Oxford: Oxford University Press.

Tomasi, D., & Volkow, N. D. (2011). Functional connectivity hubs in the human brain. *Neuroimage, 57*, 908–917.

Turkewitz, G., & Kenny, P. A. (1985). The role of developmental limitations of sensory input on sensory/perceptual organization. *Journal of Developmental and Behavioral Pediatrics, 6*, 302–306.

Turkheimer, E., Pettersson, E., & Horn, E. E. (2014). Phenotypic null hypothesis for the genetics of personality. *Annual Review of Psychology, 65*, 515–540.

Vaillend, C., Poirier, R., & Laroche, S. (2008). Genes, plasticity and mental retardation. *Behavior and Brain Research, 192*, 88–105.

van den Bergh, B. R. (2011). Developmental programming of early brain and behaviour development and mental health: A conceptual framework. *Developmental Medicine and Child Neurology, 53*, 19–23.

Vargha-Khadem, F., Carr, L. J., Isaacs, E., Brett, E., Adams, C., & Mishkin, M. (1997). Onset of speech after left hemispherectomy in a nine-year-old boy. *Brain, 120*, 159–182

Váša, F., Seidlitz, J., Romero-Garcia, R., Whitaker, K. J., Rosenthal, G., Vértes, P. E., Shinn, M., Alexander-Bloch, A., Fonagy, P., Dolan, R. J., et al. (2017). Adolescent tuning of association cortex in human structural brain networks. *Cerebral Cortex, 28*, 281–294.

Viken, R. J., Rose, R. J., Kaprio, J., & Koskenvuo, M. (1994). A developmental genetic analysis of adult personality: Extraversion and neuroticism from 18 to 59 years of age. *Journal of Personality and Social Psychology, 66*, 722–730.

Voegtline, K. M., Costigan, K. A., Pater, H. A., & DiPietro, J. A. (2013). Near-term fetal response to maternal spoken voice. *Infant Behavior and Development, 36*, 526–533.

Way, B. M., & Lieberman, M. D. (2010). Is there a genetic contribution to cultural differences? Collectivism, individualism and genetic markers of social sensitivity. *Social Cognitive and Affective Neuroscience, 5*, 203–211.

Wells, J. C. K. (2007). The thrifty phenotype as an adaptive maternal effect. *Biological Reviews, 82*, 143–172.

Werner, E. A., Myers, M. M., Fifer, W. P., Cheng, B., Fang, Y., Allen, R., & Monk, C. (2007). Prenatal predictors of infant temperament. *Developmental Psychobiology, 49*, 474–484.

Wilkinson, L. S., Davies, W., & Isles, A. R. (2007). Genomic imprinting effects on brain development and function. *Nature Reviews Neuroscience, 8*, 832–843.

Wilson, R. S. (1983). The Louisville twin study: Developmental synchronies in behavior. *Child Development, 54*, 298–316.

Winnicott, D. W. (1992). Birth memories, birth trauma, and anxiety. *International Journal of Prenatal and Perinatal Studies, 4*, 17–33.

Yecco, G. J. (1993). Neurobehavioral development and developmental support of premature infants. *The Journal of Perinatal and Neonatal Nursing, 7*, 56–65.

Yumoto, C., Jacobson, S. W., & Jacobson, J. L. (2008). Fetal substance exposure and cumulative environmental risk in an African American cohort. *Child Development, 79*, 1761–1776.

Zahir, F. R., & Brown, C. J. (2011). Epigenetic impacts on neurodevelopment: Pathophysiological mechanisms and genetic modes of action. *Pediatric Research, 69 (5 Pt 2)*, 92R–100R.

Zhang, T. Y., & Meaney, M. J. (2010). Epigenetics and the environmental regulation of the genome and its function. *Annual Review of Psychology, 61*, 439–466.

Zhong, S., He, Y., Shu, H., & Gong, G. (2017). Developmental changes in topological asymmetry between hemispheric brain white matter networks from adolescence to young adulthood. *Cerebral Cortex, 27*, 2560–2570.

Index

Locators in *italics* refer to figures and those in **bold** to tables.

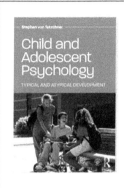

The **Topics from Child and Adolescent Psychology Series** is drawn from Stephen von Tetzchner's comprehensive textbook for all students of developmental psychology, *Child and Adolescent Psychology: Typical and Atypical Development*

Table of Contents

Praise for *Child and Adolescent Psychology: Typical and Atypical Development*

'An extensive overview of the field of developmental psychology. It illustrates how knowledge about typical and atypical development can be integrated and used to highlight fundamental processes of human growth and maturation.'

Dr. John Coleman, *PhD, OBE, UK*

'A broad panoply of understandings of development from a wide diversity of perspectives and disciplines, spanning all the key areas, and forming a comprehensive, detailed and extremely useful text for students and practitioners alike.'

Dr. Graham Music, *Consultant Psychotherapist,
Tavistock Clinic London, UK*

'An extraordinary blend of depth of scholarship with a lucid, and engaging, writing style. Its coverage is impressive . . . Both new and advanced students will love the coverage of this text.'

Professor Joseph Campos, *University of California, USA*

'Encyclopedic breadth combined with an unerring eye for the central research across developmental psychology, particularly for the period of its explosive growth since the 1960s. Both a text and a reference work, this will be the go-to resource for any teacher, researcher or student of the discipline for the foreseeable future.'

Professor Andy Lock, *University of Lisbon, Portugal*

It is accompanied by a companion website featuring chapter summaries, glossary, quizzes and instructor resources.